Tina Bruce

Early Childhood Education

4th edition

HODDER
EDUCATION
AN HACHETTE UK COMPANY

Orders: please contact Bookpoint Ltd, 130 Milton Park, Abingdon, Oxon OX14 4SB. Telephone: (44) 01235 827720. Fax: (44) 01235 400454. Lines are open from 9.00–5.00, Monday to Saturday, with a 24-hour message answering service. You can also order through our website: **www.hoddereducation.co.uk**

If you have any comments to make about this, or any of our other titles, please send them to educationenquiries@hodder.co.uk

British Library Cataloguing in Publication Data
A catalogue record for this title is available from the British Library

ISBN: 978 1 444 13714 9

First Edition Published 1987
Second Edition Published 1997
Third Edition Published 2005
This Edition Published 2011

Impression number   10 9 8 7 6 5 4 3 2 1
Year   2014, 2013, 2012, 2011

Hachette UK's policy is to use papers that are natural, renewable and recyclable products and made from wood grown in sustainable forests. The logging and manufacturing processes are expected to conform to the environmental regulations of the country of origin.

Cover photo © Fendis/Corbis.
Part 1 section header photo © xavier gallego morell – Fotolia; part 2 section header photo © Serhiy Kobyakov – Fotolia. All other photography © Andrew Callaghan, 2010.
Typeset by Pantek Arts Ltd, Maidstone, Kent.
Printed in Italy for Hodder Education, an Hachette UK Company, 338 Euston Road, London NW1 3BH.

Contents

Dedication

To Sybil Levy

The gods did not reveal, from the beginning
All things to us; in the course of time,
Through seeking, men find that which is the better.
But as for certain truth, no man has known it,
Nor will he know it; neither of the gods,
Nor yet of all things of which I speak.
And even if by chance he were to utter
The final truth, he would himself not know it;
For all is but a woven web of guesses.

Xenophanes (c. 570–475 BC)

Acknowledgements

My thanks to Colin Goodlad with whom I enjoy working and who is supportive and encouraging. Thanks to Andrew Callaghan for the photography, whose contribution has been invaluable, to Gemma Parsons who organised the photography shoots with sensitivity and skill, and to Chloé Harmsworth for her meticulous editing.

Thanks to Barbara Isaacs, Director of Studies of the Montessori Centre International, and Janni Nicol, Early Years Representative, Steiner Waldorf Education, for their insightful, helpful and fascinating dialogues with me in relation to Chapter 2. I am most grateful to Fran Paffard for her sensitively written and invaluable critical feedback, and to Sally Cave for her help with phonics as part of the reading process.

Thanks to Chris Athey, who has helped me more than I can ever say to enjoy thinking about and working with young children and their families and carers.

I have really appreciated discussions about postmodernism among other topics relating to children and families, with Hannah Bruce, Jonathan Eato, Tom and Gemma Bruce, and also with Elizabeth Bevan Roberts, who has the gift of causing thinking in very helpful ways.

I thank my parents, Margery and (the late) Peter Rowland, and my brother Marc for being loving anchors, always there for me both physically and in spirit.

Most of all, my thanks to Ian Bruce, as we continue to move together from Ruby towards Golden times, who is my best (critical) friend, who gives me real feedback, empowers me, and whose friendship I enjoy.

The author and publishers would also like to thank the following for permission to reproduce items in this book: Open Books Publishing Ltd for the illustration on page 112 taken from Goodnow, J. (1977) *Children's Drawing*; Rudolf Steiner Press for the illustrations on page 113 taken from Strauss, M. (1978) *Understanding Children's Drawings*; Heinemann Educational Books Inc., New Hampshire, for the illustrations on pages 140 and 141 taken from Ferreiro and Teberosky (1983) *Literacy Before Schooling*.

Introduction to the fourth edition of the book

Early childhood practice has undergone far-reaching changes since the first edition was written in 1987, through the impact of Conservative, New Labour and Coalition Governments.

But although governments come and governments go, the situation remains that children, as they begin to meet people beyond their family, need adults who are mature, well educated, trained and qualified to a high level in their knowledge and understanding of child development, so that they can help children to learn effectively, achieve, enjoy and make a contribution. When working with other people's children, continuing professional development is fundamental to early childhood practice and, across the years, the author has found that early childhood practitioners of different backgrounds want this. This book is offered in response to that spirit. It is heartening that this fourth edition has been requested.

In early childhood practice, we need to look to the future by building on the past. The core principles in the first edition, extrapolated from the writings of pioneer educators, especially those of Froebel, Montessori and Steiner, are, it seems, as important now, if not more so, than they were in 1987 when the first edition was published. In this fourth edition they are revisited and the practical implications will hopefully help early childhood practitioners of all kinds to make progress in the important work that they do with young children and their families.

Part 1 of this book looks at three different views of the child, three pioneer educators and, in Chapter 3, at four classic theories.

Part 2 covers the application of the principles through the creation of rich environments indoors and outdoors that are conducive to learning, schemas, representation, communication, language and literacy, how children develop understanding of the feelings and thoughts of themselves and other people, people who matter to children, diversity, inclusion and equalities, and how observation informs assessment, planning and evaluation.

The book finishes with four action points comprising an agenda for change that emphasises the socio-cultural context in which children develop and grow up, together with the biological aspects of child development and learning. These guard against stagnation and enable the contribution of the early childhood traditions to be seamlessly integrated into a continually renewed and regenerated framework for early childhood practitioners.

Early childhood education traditions: what they are and where they come from

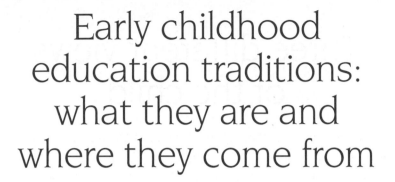

Three different views of the child

This book explores the challenges, but also reaffirms traditional approaches, to working with other people's young children and their families.

Until we are clear about the lenses through which we view children, we cannot begin to work effectively with them, nor is it easy to work in partnership with other practitioners or multi-agency colleagues, parents or carers, because our assumptions about the child are crucial in influencing our practice.

The most typical lenses through which early childhood practitioners have viewed, and continue to view, the child are:

* **The empiricist lens**. Looking through this lens, the child is seen as an empty vessel to be filled or a lump of clay to be moulded by adults into the desired shape. This derives from the philosophy of John Locke (1632–1704).
* **The nativist lens**. This is the opposite of the empiricist approach. The nativist practitioner sees the child as pre-programmed to unfold in certain directions. This is influenced by the philosopher Jean-Jacques Rousseau (1712–1778).
* **The interactionist view**. Children are seen partly as empty vessels and partly as pre-programmed. There is an interaction within and between the two. Immanuel Kant (1724–1804) originated this approach.

Empiricism – transmitting the culture

John Locke (1632–1704)

John Locke grew up near Bristol; he was educated at Westminster School and the University of Oxford, where he studied medicine. His education was sponsored by a senior officer serving in the Parliamentarian army during the English Civil War under the command of Locke's father.

Locke believed in religious tolerance and freedom of belief, and that lack of this results in more violence than allowing diversity. He pioneered the idea that humans have a self, which is in the body, reached through the physical senses (hearing, seeing, smelling, tasting, touching and moving) and which has continuity throughout life. However, he put forward the notion that at birth the human is a tabula rasa (a blank) and that experience is crucial in influencing whether or not a person develops good or bad associations. He wrote about this in 'An essay concerning human understanding', which was heavily influenced, as the thinking of seventeenth-century philosophers often was, by Islamic texts from the twelfth century. It is not surprising that he emphasised the impact of education during childhood in 'Some thoughts concerning education and of the conduct of understanding'.

The empiricist view of education sees the child as a tabula rasa, empty vessel or vessel to be filled. This implicitly subscribes to a deficit model of the child. The role of the adult emphasises the identification of missing experiences, skills, concepts, and so on, and the adult selects appropriate experiences and transmits them to the child. This orientation came to the fore during the compensatory education movement of the late 1960s, with Bereiter and Engelmann as clear proponents. This work built on the work of psychologists such as Watson (1878–1958) and Skinner (1904–1990). In 1925 Watson wrote:

> … give me a dozen healthy infants, well-formed and my own special world to bring them up in and I will guarantee to take any one at random and train him to become any type of specialist. I might select doctor, lawyer, artist, merchant-chief and, yes, even beggarman and thief – regardless of his talents, penchants, tendencies, abilities and vocation and race of his ancestors.
>
> (In Schaffer, 1996: 20)

This quote demonstrates how, in this approach, children are seen as something to be moulded into shape and given experiences that are appropriate and necessary for them to take their place in society. Habit formation is valued and learning is broken down into meaningful sequences; for example, children are taught step by step to tie their shoes, hold their knives and forks correctly, sing songs that are part of their heritage, know their letters and numbers, and so on. In the early childhood tradition, empiricism has always held a place. John Locke's influence is not as great in this tradition as it might have been, because he emphasised the importance of learning through the senses. His alphabet blocks can still be found today, with raised letters on the faces for children to hold, feel, see, suck, bang together and balance, giving movement feedback through the body. But the empiricist approach has tended to become more linked with paper-and-pencil learning, rather than first experiences through the senses, albeit chosen, controlled and led by the adult.

Depending on whether we support the view of the child as passive recipient of culture and knowledge, or as an active explorer and initiator of experiences, the adult's role in working with that child will completely change. In other words, there may be agreement that the child is shaped by events, situations, objects or people that he or she meets, but there is disagreement over the nature of those experiences.

Empiricist approach – key aspects

* The child is likened to an empty vessel to be filled, a lump of clay to be moulded into shape, or blotting paper that absorbs the ink poured onto it.
* Habit formation is seen as important, for example practising handwriting with correct pencil grip or lining up in an orderly way ready for playtime.
* Children are taught in small, simple steps and cannot proceed to the next one until each is mastered in turn.
* Learning is seen as a hierarchy from simple to complex.
* Knowledge of the culture is seen as something that needs to be transmitted from adult to child.
* The adult is seen as needing always to lead the child's learning and to dominate and control it (guiding).

CASE STUDY

The teacher decides to make bread with the children after reading the story of the 'Little Red Hen'. She collects the ingredients and equipment needed as part of planning for the activity. She organises a rota of groups, so that each child has a turn at making bread. She begins each group session by demonstrating a stage in the bread making and then hands the bowl round for each child to have a turn. She comments on the key elements of successful mixing, or measuring, and so on. In this way the task is completed through simple steps. The children watch the teacher place the bread in the oven, and take it out when cooked. She cuts the loaf, and each child has a piece of bread to eat. Children say if they want butter or not. The story of the 'Little Red Hen' is told again at the end of the week when all the children have had a turn at bread making. Children can take a recipe card home to make bread with their family if they wish.

While a group of children takes part in cooking, other children are involved in tasks set by the teacher. They complete these at a table, or work with the Teaching Assistant.

The following week the teacher checks how much the children have remembered about bread making, by asking questions and giving them work sheets to fill in. Those with correct answers receive a star. The children are then placed in groups according to how well they have performed (although the teacher believes that the children do not realise the nature of the groups).

The teacher has chosen the topic, and leads the experience of the children. She checks on the knowledge that has been transmitted. Do the children know how to make bread? Do they know the story of the 'Little Red Hen'?

Nativism – biologically pre-programmed to learn naturally

Jean-Jacques Rousseau (1712–1778)

Rousseau grew up in Geneva but moved away in later childhood. He was a major influence on the thinking of the French and American Revolutions. He had four children with Therese Levasseur. He came to the view that mothers should remove swaddling clothes and breastfeed their own babies, rather than send them away to a wet nurse. This, ironically (for his own children were sent to a foundling hospital), probably saved the lives of thousands of children. He believed that humans are happier when they are compassionate and show empathy for others, when they show reason through seeing and acting on the consequences of their actions. This leads to the development of a civil society.

The nativist or biologically pre-programmed view of the child suggests that humans are biologically pre-programmed with a propensity to unfold in certain ways. Bower (1974: 2) describes the nativist view 'that human knowledge and human skill were built into the structure of the organism'. Rousseau would also say the desire to be good is part of this. Typical supporters of this stance would be Gesell, Erikson (a psychodynamic theorist) and, more recently, Chomsky. For Gesell (1954: 13), growth is seen as being

> … laid down by intrinsic patterning prior to and independent of actual experience … environment predicts preliminary patterns; it determines the occasion, the intensity and the correlation of many aspects of behaviour development, but it does not engender the basic progressive behaviour development. These are determined by inherent maturational mechanisms.

Sally (aged one year) begins to walk when she is ready, not before, holding the armchairs and moving further and further from one to the other in the room. This view is supported by Erikson (1963: 11), 'If we only learn to let live, the plan for growth is all there.' Chomsky reasserts this stance when he claims that we have an innate propensity for language. The environment dictates the kind of language learned, but the Language Acquisition Device (LAD) is, he argues, a genetic part of being a human.

In the nativist tradition there remains a feeling that adults might interfere in a child's learning by intervening in the wrong way at an inappropriate moment. Rousseau's concept of natural justice is evident. Children naturally learn from their actions in his view. The nativist approach emphasises that children need to play, develop creatively and with imagination, uninterrupted by interfering adults. Adults can offer help, but in this approach they should never insist upon it. They need to be highly skilled in the way they approach children.

The home area in an early years setting is still often a sacrosanct area with walls around it so that children can be away from adults in a 'world of their own'. Inevitably this leads to a major emphasis on relationships between adults and peers, based on respect for the child's unfolding development. These assertions stem from the nativist influence on the early childhood tradition.

Nativism – key aspects

* The child is pre-programmed for development to unfold, and this unfolding is determined by genetically pre-programmed maturational mechanisms.
* The socio-cultural aspects influence, for example, the language(s) a child speaks. If a child hears Chinese, then the child learns to speak that language, but the mechanisms for learning language are already there.
* In this approach, there is great emphasis on adults observing children and monitoring progress, with attention paid to milestones. Readiness checks are made, in relation to physical development or learning to read.
* The child is seen as leading his or her own learning, with the adult as the facilitator.

The inadequacies of extreme versions of empiricism or nativism

Empiricism and nativism are two lenses that, because they see the child so differently, should lead to entirely different ways of working with young children. In a sense, however, despite the great differences between them ideologically, they are often more polarised in theory than they are in practice (Bruce, 1984; Bruce, Findlay, Read and Scarborough, 1995). This may well be because of the inadequacy of the theoretical support that either of these approaches alone can give to early childhood practice. In the practical setting, people have to get on with the job in the absence of satisfactory theoretical support for their work.

Both stances have, in fact, exerted strong influences over the early childhood traditions, but in many respects they present diametrically opposed ways of viewing the child. It is no wonder that there is confusion and a lack of articulation about how the aims of that tradition can be reached in practice. If early childhood practice is to move forward, which it needs to do, more adequate ways of viewing the child's development and learning are needed that are not embedded in culturally narrow, obsolete or incomplete theories.

Certainly the nativist view of the child has had its periods of ascendancy, especially in Europe, and empiricism has had periods of dominance, primarily in the USA but also more recently in England. However, in reality, the early childhood traditions are capable of embracing a much more complex approach than either of these two polarised approaches. In fact, the early childhood tradition is too complex for one to say that it sees the child from a dominantly empiricist or a nativist viewpoint.

Interactionism – a little like having conversations, dancing together or making music together

Immanuel Kant (1724–1804)

Immanuel Kant was a philosopher who influenced Enlightenment ideas. He lived in Konigsberg in Prussia and never went further than ten miles from his home. Yet his thinking has had influence worldwide, including his contribution to the study of astronomy. He emphasised the importance of understanding the beginnings and the limits of human knowledge, the structures of the mind, and the crucial role of direct and real experience in the development of thinking. In his view, our thoughts are the result of how our minds are structured to think, but they are also limited by those structures. These a priori structures give the form of the mind, and are about time, space and reasons in particular. He gave an important place to causality (cause-and-effect relationships as aspects of reasoning) and the development in understanding of time and space. These, he believed, are central features of the developing intellect.

He developed the idea of concepts as categories of understanding. Through these, people are able to be active and do their own thinking. Our experiences (the content of our learning) are formed through the senses. He calls this a posteriori learning, which depends on experience. Seeing, hearing, touching, tasting, smelling and movement feedback, and our minds then process what is experienced, giving order and understanding through the concepts in the mind. He wrote two books that are landmarks in the history of philosophy. *A Critique of Pure Reason* is one. The other is *A Critique of Practical Reason*, in which he wrote:

> Two things fill the mind with ever new and increasing admiration and awe, the more often and steadily we reflect upon them: the starry heavens above me and the moral law within me.

He saw people as active, rational thinkers about moral issues.

In the interactionist view of the child, which is influenced by the philosophy of Kant, not only do the biological structures in the child's brain interact with each other, but they also alter each other in the light of the people they meet and the cultural and physical experiences they have (Bruce, 2004). There is interaction with what is external, but there is also interaction within the child through the senses and through the interconnectivity of different parts of the brain. This is a much more sophisticated view of the child. It is gaining ever-increasing evidence to support it (Bruce, 2004), through cognitive psychology (Mandler, Forman), connectionists (Bates, Karmiloff-Smith), the neurosciences (Greenfield, 2000; Trevarthen, 2002; Dennett, 2003; Damasio, 2004) and social constructivism (Athey, 1990), and is also supported by socio-cultural strands in the research (Rogoff *et al.*, 1993). It places emphasis on the socio-cultural context in which children grow up, develop and learn, as much as on the biological path of their development. Damasio (2004: 37) gives the image of 'a tall messy tree with progressively higher and more elaborate branches coming out of the main trunks, and this maintains a two-way communication with their roots'. He calls this the 'nesting principle' through which 'parts of simpler reactions are incorporated as components of more elaborate ones, a nesting of the simple within the complex'.

In the interactionist approach, children are not seen as nativist sole instigators of their knowledge, pre-programmed to learn naturally, and held back or helped as the case may be by variations in the environment and culture. They are instead supported by adults and other children, who help them to make maximum use of the environment and cultural setting.

This implicitly reasserts the view of pioneers of the early childhood traditions (Chapter 2) that the role of the adult is critical. Adults are not seen as empiricist instructors giving out information and knowledge. Instead, they are seen as the means, the mechanism, by which children can develop their own strategies, initiatives and responses, and construct their own rules that enable their development.

But earlier theories (Kant lived before scientific theories developed) also give support to the interactionist approach, and they chime with the philosophy of Kant in important ways. Piaget (1896–1980) trained as a zoologist, studying water snails and publishing many important scientific papers on the subject by the age of 21 years. He became interested in genetic epistemology, the study of how knowledge develops in human beings. He realised the importance of early childhood for later development. His work resonates with Kant's ideas in that he realised that in young children there are schemas, which are structures in the brain that serve as windows on the world. These, as they develop, become concepts. Like Kant he focused on an understanding of Time, Space and Reasoning (Causality) as central to the development of thinking. He also emphasised the way children learn through the senses, and that the mind processes real and direct experiences, with the increasing possibility of thinking in ways less tied to the here and now. Piaget's work is explored in more depth in the next chapter, together with that of Vygotsky and Bruner.

Although Lev Vygotsky (1896–1934) was born in the same year as Piaget, he died of tuberculosis at an early age. His work was not translated into English until the 1960s. His criticisms of the work of Piaget were, by then, out of date, as Piaget's work had moved on. Piaget regretted not having had the opportunity to meet him. Piaget acknowledged that Vygotsky was right in his assertion that when children (typically at about five years of age) talk to themselves, they are engaged in private speech. Like Kant, Vygotsky saw real experience of the material world and people as feeding the mind, such that the interpersonal is first and then the inner life develops, with more abstract thinking becoming possible. He, like Piaget, placed great emphasis on language being crucial for abstract thinking, but he placed greater importance on language before this, seeing it as part of early experience of the world and the culture. His work is in tune with

Figure 1.1: Interactionism is a bit like a conversation: each participant is interested in and engages with what the other one finds fascinating.

that of Kant in that he investigated thought, reasoning and logical memory. There is a resonance with Kant in the Marxian attention Vygotsky paid to collectivism, cooperation and sharing. Kant explored the concept of duty, and the categorical imperative (which looks at the demands of moral law on individuals).

Jerome Bruner (1915–) is interesting because in many ways he bridges the work of Piaget and Vygotsky. As we shall see in the next chapter, the three theories of Piaget, Vygotsky and Bruner make a powerful trio when put together. Although there are differences between them, they are all in the interactionist framework. Bruner's work also has resonance with Kant's philosophy. He sees the mind as processing knowledge, and having structures through which to achieve this. Kant states that pure reason without experience is of no value and that thinking requires a context, based in real life, so that it is practical reasoning. Bruner has increasingly explored this aspect, emphasising the importance of culture and social relationships. Piaget is closer to Kant than either Vygotsky or Bruner in this respect, in that he focuses more on the material, physical world of the senses and active movement. But they all agree on the importance of real and direct experience in the company of others.

The key to the interactionist approach in early childhood education lies in the notion of reciprocity, or give and take; this means that sometimes the child leads and sometimes the adult leads

Colwyn Trevarthen (2003), over many years, has studied proto-conversations between adults and babies, and has shown the importance of give and take (reciprocity) in these. Conversations are not monologues by adults, issuing instructions or asking children questions to which the adult knows the answer.

Both Damasio and Trevarthen emphasise the interactionist ways in which the brain communicates both with itself (internally) and with other people and situations (externally).

Work by Trevarthen (2002, 2003) and colleagues (Malloch and Trevarthen, 2009) with musicians shows how the musical rhythm of the conversation between babies and carers means that babies participate with a particular rhythm and beat with unerring accuracy when their mother talks with them.

Similarly Siraj-Blatchford and colleagues (EPPE, 2003) have shown how important it is that adults do not dominate in conversations between adults and children, but are involved in shared focus and exchanges of ideas and feelings. They call these 'shared, sustained thinking'.

The Effective Provision of Pre-School Education (EPPE, 2003) shows how important it is that adults tune in to what children say, and respond in the light of this, as happens when conversations feel good to those making them together.

These research and development studies support the view of the pioneer educators. In short, the interactionist view of the child supports the main principles of the early childhood traditions that will be considered in Chapter 2.

The aim in this book is not to preserve a 'one size fits all' approach to work with young children, using the banner of 'universals' to do so, which, as we shall see in the last part of this chapter, has been criticised by Dahlberg *et al.* (1999) and other postmodernists. Instead the aim is to conserve that which is found to be worthwhile and effective, and to build upon it. This means conservation of what is effective, and not just romantic preservation of the traditional.

The EPPE research, directed by Kathy Sylva (EPPE, 2003), shows that in England the most effective provision is in integrated centres and maintained nursery schools. Since nearly 60 per cent of the integrated centres are adapted nursery schools, with graduate-trained nursery teachers, this really suggests that this traditional form of practice has sustained its record of excellence across a hundred years, and across constantly changing socio-cultural contexts.

It is also important to assess the heritage of early childhood work in different cultures and in different parts of the world. The interpretation of core principles will vary, for example in Finland, New Zealand, South America, the USA, Indonesia or India, in both the broad sense and also in the interpretation of individual early childhood specialists who may vary in their outlook, even within a culture.

The interactionist view is a broad one within which there is inevitably a measure of debate and lack of agreement. It nevertheless gives present-day support to the early childhood traditions, both in theoretical ways and through research evidence.

Interactionism – key aspects

* This approach integrates empiricism and nativism, recognising that there are biological predispositions to develop movement, communication, language, representation, symbol use, attachment to people, and so on, in children. There is also a heavy emphasis on the socio-cultural context in which the child grows up, comprising people, and cultural and physical environments.
* The context is understood to be diverse in its range in different parts of the world, and in different families and communities.
* People are important, both children and adults. Sometimes one leads, sometimes another.
* Interactionism is a little like a conversation. Different people might start conversations, but the various speakers need to listen to each other and respond in the light of what the other person has said, appropriately and relevantly.
* Interactionism is also a little like dancing together or making music together. People have to 'tune in to' each other, be sensitive to what others do and respond appropriately.

Figure 1.2: The key to the interactionist approach in early childhood education lies in the notion of reciprocity. Sometimes the child initiates and leads, and sometimes the adult initiates and leads, but the main thing is that each engages with and tunes in to the other.

Postmodernism and the traditions of early childhood education

Fran Paffard suggests that:

> Postmodernism as a movement has been influential in the worlds of philosophy and the arts but has also had some influence on early years ideas. It could be argued that the contribution of postmodernism is not creative. It deconstructs rather than constructs, but has provided a challenge to established ways of thinking.
>
> (Paffard, 2011)

Debbie Albon (in Miller and Pound, 2010: 38) argues that:

> the key contribution postmodernist thinking has made to early childhood education and care is in disrupting commonly held 'truths' about our understandings of children and how they develop and learn and, consequently, the curricula and pedagogical approaches practitioners employ in early childhood settings.

The traditions of early childhood education are rooted in a particular western history philosophy and culture, and Fran Paffard argues:

> This challenge to established truths can be a salutary reminder to practitioners to examine their preconceptions and prejudices and to gain perspective on the roots of their own philosophy. The postmodern movement in early years has, to some extent, become confused with the rise in prominence of an equalities agenda that emphasises the need to acknowledge the very different socio-cultural contexts that our diverse children operate in.
>
> (Paffard, 2011)

Antjie Krog (in *A Change of Tongue*, 2003: 256) writes:

> Someone who had visited [Nelson Mandela] asked me why he repeats some of his stories word for word, just as they have been written down … It has nothing to do with old age. It's very deliberate. Mandela is doing it intentionally … to undermine what he calls the whole postmodernist notion of ever changing texts.

Developmental psychology has always, as Debbie Albon (in Miller and Pound, 2010: 45) says, argued that children are not, when very young, as autonomous or competent as they are later able to become, with appropriate help and support. They are therefore vulnerable and dependent when young. Postmodernism ignores this in her view. There is also little acknowledgement of the physical, relational or developing self. Instead, it is argued that the self is ever changing, which is different.

However, as Fran Paffard points out:

> The postmodern concern with language may encourage us to debate our terminology but can also result in a morass of jargon that obscurates more than it reveals, and is ultimately unproductive. At best, postmodernism encourages us to think 'outside our boxes' and consider alternatives to our strongly held beliefs, and to tolerate a level of uncertainty. At worst, it creates a moral vacuum in which children are particularly vulnerable.

> Since postmodernism problematises rather than creates, its influence has been more on ideas than practice. It could also be said that we are now in a post postmodern era in which the need for some nailing of colours to the mast has been recognised, and to know what we will do tomorrow!
>
> (Paffard, 2011)

The next chapter looks at the principles of the early childhood tradition and examines the work of three pioneers of early childhood education – Froebel, Montessori and Steiner – through the interactionist view. Using this lens, it is possible to give their thoughts considerable support theoretically, although it is necessary to update the terminology that surrounds their work.

Ten principles of the pioneers: the bedrock of the early childhood traditions

This chapter looks at three of the most influential pioneers of early childhood practice in the UK, and draws out commonalities between them that form some bedrock principles both in the UK and beyond. They are Friedrich Wilhelm Froebel (1782–1852), Maria Montessori (1869–1952) and Rudolf Steiner (1861–1925). Each has an international reputation and influence. Each has influenced schools, which claim to use their approaches, in different parts of the world. Each has training courses where practitioners learn about their ideas. Most importantly, each has significantly influenced mainstream education in Europe and North America. All three were skilled practitioners as well as being educational theorists. Each was concerned, among other things, with world citizenship, respect for individual needs, poverty and the concept of community.

Other pioneer educators, such as Pattie Smith Hill (USA, 1868–1946), Margaret McMillan (UK, 1860–1931) and Susan Isaacs (UK, 1885–1948), each working in the Froebelian tradition, have also been influential in contributing to these common principles and traditions, but not across all the criteria mentioned above. The same can be said of the Reggio Emilia approach, pioneered by Loris Malaguzzi (1920–1994).

The work of these pioneer educators with young children and their families reveals a set of common principles that have endured and still have a useful future. The agreements and disagreements between them have been fundamental in creating our early childhood traditions. The emphasis in this book is on keeping the heritage in the spirit of conservation, not preservation and ossification, as discussed in the previous chapter. The early childhood traditions embrace diversity, rather than fragmentation, standardisation and uniformity.

The early pioneers used language that is difficult to understand today, and this means that their common principles and important differences have become obscured. It is important to identify when differences of value become irreconcilable, or when values are shared but their practical interpretation is different.

The need to revisit, rework and own the core principles of practice in early childhood work is demonstrated by reframing the wording of 1987 into more current wording. In the first edition of this book (Bruce, 1987) the ten common principles were quoted as follows:

1. Childhood is seen as valid in itself, as part of life and not simply as preparation for adulthood. Thus education is seen similarly as something of the present and not just preparation and training for later.
2. The whole child is considered to be important. Health – physical and mental – is emphasised, as well as the importance of feelings and thinking and spiritual aspects.
3. Learning is not compartmentalised, for everything links.
4. Intrinsic motivation, resulting in child-initiated, self-directed activity, is valued.
5. Self-discipline is emphasised.
6. There are specially receptive periods of learning at different stages of development.
7. What children can do (rather than what they cannot do) is the starting point in the child's education.
8. There is an inner life in the child that emerges especially under favourable conditions.
9. The people (both adults and children) with whom the child interacts are of central importance.
10. The child's education is seen as an interaction between the child and the environment in which the child finds itself – including, in particular, other people and knowledge itself.

The ten bedrock principles revisited and reframed are as follows:

1. The best way to prepare children for their adult life is to give them what they need as children.
2. Children are whole people who have feelings, ideas, a sense of embodied self and relationships with others, and who need to be physically, mentally, morally and spiritually healthy.
3. Areas of learning involving the humanities, arts and sciences cannot be separated; young children learn in an integrated way and not in neat, tidy compartments.
4. Children learn best when they are given appropriate responsibility, allowed to experiment, make errors, decisions and choices, and are respected as autonomous learners.
5. Self-discipline is emphasised as the only kind of discipline worth having. Reward systems are very short term and do not work in the long term in developing the moral and spiritual aspects of living. Children need their efforts to be valued and appreciated.
6. There are times when children are especially able to learn particular things.
7. What children can do (rather than what they cannot do) is the starting point for a child's learning.
8. Diverse kinds of symbolic behaviour develop and emerge when learning environments conducive to this are created at home, in early childhood settings, indoors and outdoors.

9. Relationships with other people (both adults and children) are of central importance in a child's life, influencing emotional and social well-being.

10. Quality education is about three things: the child, the context in which learning takes place, and the knowledge and understanding that the child develops and learns.

In the next section of this chapter the ten common principles are taken in turn, with reference to the interactionist philosophies of Froebel, Montessori and Steiner.

1 The best way to prepare children for their adult life is to give them what they need as children

Froebel, Montessori and Steiner agree that early childhood is not merely a period when children are prepared and trained for adult life. It is a phase of life that is important in its own right although, as a by-product, the more richly that childhood is experienced the more strongly the adult phase can be entered. Giving children what they need during childhood is the best preparation for adulthood.

Froebel saw the family as the most important first educator in the child's life. Joachim Liebschner (1985: 35) points out that Froebel believed women were important not only in their role as parents but were capable of teaching children too. This was a revolutionary idea at that time! The school was seen as a community, where home and school came together. Parents were seen as part of the community. Froebel (1887: 89) said, 'Let us live with our children, let them live with us, so shall we gain through them what all of us need.'

Children and adults learn from each other and through each other, and enrich each other's lives. Children are not seen as being in need of instruction in how to achieve an all-knowing adulthood. Childhood is seen as a different state from adulthood, one that takes from and gives to the community in its own way (Bruce *et al.*, 1995: 18).

Montessori also recognised the different nature of childhood. Again, she did not see the role of the adult as preparing children for adulthood. But she did not emphasise the parents as part of the prepared environment. Instead she saw childhood as a state to be protected and allowing children to develop without damage in a specially prepared environment. In *The Secret of Childhood* (1966) she describes this as a favourable rather than a prepared environment

> that protects the child from the difficult and dangerous obstacles that threaten him/her in the adult world. The shelter in the storm, the oasis in the desert, the place of spiritual rest ought to be created in the world precisely to assure the healthy development of the child.
>
> (Montessori, 1966: 13)

The name Casa dei Bambini (The Children's House) contrasts with Froebel's Kindergarten, symbolising a protected, predictable, contained environment as well as a controlled environment. It is cocoon-like, and may reflect her relationship with her son. She wants other children to have what she has not been able to give Mario.

She argued that 'the child is a personality separate from the adult'. Children need different treatment but not, for Montessori, in the Froebelian sense of community where adults 'live with their children'. Montessori argued instead for a favourable environment where adults do not enter the child's world except for the trained directress who 'liberates' the child. Childhood is seen as a state with needs quite separate from those of adult life, existing in its own right. The emphasis is more on the individual child, whereas for Froebel the child is respected as an individual, but relationships with other children and with adults are at the heart of the learning community.

For Steiner also there is no question of childhood simply preparing children for adulthood. Again, childhood exists as a period of life in its own right. In his philosophy, life after death is seen as another aspect of life before birth. There is therefore no question of childhood being 'preparation for life' but rather the idea of helping the child to find his or her way in this life. Janni Nicol, who is the Early Childhood Representative for the Steiner Waldorf Schools Fellowship, emphasises that Steiner talks of three phases of childhood:

> In the first (birth to 7 years), the child is inclined to respond to his world through the 'will' (directed movement) and is highly sensitive to his or her environment. The spirituality of the child is held in the highest regard, therefore the child's entry into the world needs to be protected and the environment is therefore carefully planned. While the adult can offer a certain resistance to his environment, the child accepts it, drinks it in. Thus the whole environment of the child should be a positive, harmonious one.
>
> (Wilkinson, in Bruce, 1997b)

In the second phase (7–14 years) children live strongly in the emotional realm, and the teaching methods address their feeling for life. In the third phase (14–21) the adolescent enters the realms of ideas and ideal. This is a fusion of head (thinking), heart (feeling) and will (doing) – an education of the mind, body and spirit. This 'threefoldness' of body, soul and spirit is acknowledged.

Steiner, like Montessori, separated the child from the world during the first seven years, and placed him or her in a carefully planned environment. Montessori and Steiner differ from Froebel who, while he also saw childhood as a stage with its own needs, distinct from adulthood, nevertheless saw the child as being in the community and the school as within that community. Children are not seen by Froebel as in need of protection from their community. Instead, they are seen as being part of it, and contributing to it from the birth, and possibly before then. None of them saw childhood as simply preparation for adult life. Froebel, Montessori and Steiner all saw childhood as a part of life, with its own particular needs and requirements, which are important in their own right. Their interpretations are entirely different, though. Shared principles do not lead to shared practice.

2 Children are whole people who have feelings, ideas, a sense of embodied self and relationships with others, and who need to be physically, mentally, morally and spiritually healthy

Froebel, Montessori and Steiner all considered the development of the whole child to be of enormous importance.

Froebel saw the whole child as including the physical, spiritual, feeling and intellectual aspects of the person. Like Montessori and Steiner, he gave a great deal of thought to how the whole child could be developed through an appropriate curriculum. His invented the 'kindergarten' (the garden of children) in 1839, which partly emphasises nature, partly community and partly family (Bruce *et al.*, 1995).

Froebel addressed himself to the physical needs of the child through the 'forms of life', which involved the senses and first-hand experiences, to the feelings, creativity, expressiveness and imagination of the child through the 'forms of beauty' – music, arts and crafts, nature and mathematics. He addressed himself to the thinking, ideas and problem-solving abilities of the child through the 'forms of knowledge'. The moral and spiritual pervades everything (Liebschner, 1991, 1992). This approach does not separate the different aspects of the child's learning. It integrates learning. The concept of 'unity' in learning is central to the Froebelian approach, demonstrating the interconnectedness of learning for both children and adults.

In his earlier work Froebel approached this through his 'Mother Songs' (1878), 'Gifts', 'Occupations', 'Movement Games' and the garden (1887). Every experience presented to the child was presented first as a whole. The first Gift was the soft sphere; the second Gift was the cube, cylinder and wooden sphere; the third, fourth, fifth and sixth Gifts were cubes divided in different ways, comprising small wooden blocks (bricks) that could be built into a larger one. Only after being presented whole were they broken down into parts. The whole preceded the parts.

Later, Froebel moved increasingly away from a set curriculum and became more interested in the process of play in the child, which he began to see as the mediator between opposing forces: the natural and spiritual, emotion and intellect. In other words, he saw play as a means by which the child maintains the wholeness (the unity) of his or her experiences (Bruce, 1987, 1991, 1996).

Play is a unifying mechanism and, for this reason, it was for Froebel the highest level of learning. It was the most spiritual activity of the child in that it gave meaning to relationship with self, others and the universe. For him no single aspect in development was more important than any other. The whole child is the child where all aspects of development are enabled and deep learning results.

While Montessori believed equally strongly in the whole child, she approached the concept quite differently. Rather than Froebel's views of the interconnected wholeness of learning, she created a simple-to-complex hierarchical model. Each sense is developed separately and in isolation (visual, aural, baric (weight) learning and so on) through a sequence of carefully graded, simple-to-complex, separated out, sensorial exercises. The focus is on one sense at a time. She considered that, as children master each step and arrive at the end of a sequence, they are then in a position to use, in a general way, the skills acquired:

> but, once the handicraft leading to the construction of vases has been learned (and this is part of the progress in the work learned from the direct and graduated instruction of the teacher), anyone can modify it according to the inspiration of his aesthetic tastes, and this is the artistic, individual part of the work.
>
> (Montessori, 1912: 22)

Montessori took each part of the child's development and built it to make the whole through her simple-to-complex model (Bruce, 1984). Barbara Isaacs (personal communication, 2004) sees 'her preoccupation with carefully structured activities as based on her belief that the child "scaffolds" his or her learning through these activities'. She suggests that Montessori sees the role of the adult as fundamentally different in practical life and sensorial aspects from mathematics and literacy, which 'reflects the child's growing ability to communicate his or her ideas, and have a discussion or follow instructions, whereas in practical life and sensorial exercises the child finds it easier to learn by imitation'.

In most respects, Montessori's view of the whole child contrasts with that of Froebel. However, Barbara Isaacs sees some inconsistency in Montessori's approach in that, although in the main she advocates working from the simple to the complex, when looking at the world she embraces the 'cosmic' approach (a term borrowed from Froebel) (in Standing, 1957: 362), where she wanted the child to feel part of the whole cosmos and to learn about the planets and Earth, before learning about continents and countries. This global perspective supports her argument for peace education.

Montessori was, initially, deeply influenced by Froebel, but she moved away in most respects from his concept of the unity that is in all learning. Froebel began with the whole and then the parts, and for Montessori, all but one aspects (the cosmos) started with the part before the whole. Montessorians have embraced the current emphasis on teaching synthetic phonics, since this involves the smallest sound (the phoneme). This is easy to teach in Italian, which was Montessori's language. In Chapter 7 a Froebelian emphasis is given, in which, supported by researchers such as Usha Goswami, the syllable, rhyming chunk and then phoneme are introduced (whole to part). This works better in English and many other world languages.

Steiner was also concerned with the whole child. He believed that we bring various qualities with us into life. The whole child emerges as the four-fold picture of man (Steiner, 1965: 21) involving the physical body, the life body, the soul element and individuality. Uneven development is seen as damaging.

> It is always a matter of balance in human values. An all-round harmonious development is the first aim, furtherance of special talent can come later.
>
> (Wilkinson, in Bruce, 1997b)

Like Montessori, Steiner believed that children learn mainly through imitation. It is important to tease out the Froebelian meaning of this word, and that of Montessori and Steiner. For Froebelians (see Chapter 6) it means reproducing something in a different context because the imitation is embedded and has meaning which is then applied. For Montessorians and Steinerians there is a closer link to copying. The child repeats what the adult does, and may not generalise this to other situations. Jill Tina Taplin suggests that, for Steiner, 'The adult stands before the child as an example, modelling to the child ways of managing day-to-day life that will be absorbed by the child. This avoids direct instruction.' Teaching by example is the preferred Steiner approach (*up to the age of 7 years*) because it does not stimulate the child's intellect, but allows him or her to spend their time in a mood of unselfconscious participation.

Steiner saw the child as a visible entity, possessing an invisible, inner soul life and an eternal spiritual nature. Steiner was like both Froebel and Montessori in that he placed great emphasis on processes in the child. Steiner considered that the whole is reflected in each of its parts. In this respect he was more like Froebel than Montessori. The whole comes first. (This is unlike Montessori's simple-to-complex hierarchical model.) Although Froebel, Montessori and Steiner all emphasised the whole child, they interpreted this very differently, with the result being very different in practice.

> ## 3 Areas of learning involving the humanities, arts and sciences cannot be separated; young children learn in an integrated way and not in neat, tidy compartments

In the previous section, emphasis on the whole child was highlighted. In this section the wholeness of knowledge and the fact that everything connects is stressed. Nothing can be compartmentalised. Froebel (1887: 128) believed that:

> The school endeavours to render the scholar fully conscious of the nature and inner life of things and of himself and teach him to know the inner relations of things to one another, to the human being, scholar and living source and conscious unity of all things.

This 'conscious unity of all things' was central to Froebel's philosophy. He saw a unity between home and school, and community and nature, and between different areas of knowledge. We saw in the previous section the links between different aspects of the child's development. Froebel (1887: 134) said:

> Never forget that the essential business of the school is not so much to teach, but to communicate the variety and multiplicity of all things as it is to give prominence to the everlasting unity that is in all things.

The soft ball (the first Gift) contrasts with and contradicts the wooden ball (the second Gift). In Froebel's notion of a sequence, there is not a smooth progression but slight changes in the familiar, since learning involves challenges to what is already known. This has important implications later in this book (Chapter 10) when differences and common features in people are focused upon (Bruce *et al.*, 1995).

In both this section and the last, Froebel's approach to the whole and to unity across different aspects of the whole is stressed. Everything relates and connects. In the same way Montessori's simple-to-complex model can be applied both to her view of the whole child and to links within and between knowledge. For Montessori, the links are gradually built, step by step, and a complicated world is thereby carefully made comprehensible. For example, through the use of didactic materials, or the carefully sequenced exercises of practical life, she emphasised imitation. She isolated each sense, and developed each sense independently – baric, thermic, visual and so on – 'from the education of the senses to general notions, from general notions to abstract thought, from abstract thought to morality' (Montessori, 1912: 4). In her approach to mathematics and literacy she emphasised discussion and following instructions.

Steiner's notion of unity is more like Froebel's in that he wanted to help children towards the essential unity by formulating a network across different areas of knowledge and different stages of development, which would illuminate unifying concepts in different contexts.

In the early years of modern approaches to Steiner (Waldorf) education, as Lynne Oldfield (2003) shows in detail in her book, *Free to Learn*, there is emphasis on the use of working with ecology, rhythm and repetition as aids to learning, about the seasons and festivals, and embracing diversity and the outdoors. For instance, justice was explored in early education through the child's temperament, balanced by activity and imitation. This is done with the help of the early years worker who is a warm parent figure. Later, it is explored through the history of the Romans, and later still through the notion of justice as an idea, with the Romans as one example of a culture to be compared and analysed alongside others. For Steiner, natural science, literature, mathematics – indeed all areas of knowledge – link and (as seen in the previous section) so do the different facets of the child's development.

Both Froebel and Steiner saw links between subjects and between different aspects of the child's development as beginning with the home. Montessori reached the whole through the parts in a separate 'prepared' environment. Froebel did not stipulate a particular order and method in the way experiences are offered to the child; his later emphasis on play moved him steadily away from this.

Later in this chapter, this idea will become important, as it leads towards an informally structured interactionist approach to early childhood. Barbara Isaacs (personal communication, 2004) points out that 'Montessori, like Froebel, advocated that adults need to develop the skill of knowing how and when to intervene in the child's learning … However, her hierarchical model encourages some adults to work with children in a more controlling manner.' This, in her view, is something that can be addressed through the training of Montessori practitioners. Froebelians would argue that it is intrinsic to the simple-to-complex approach dominating the Montessorian method.

Montessori and Steiner helped the child towards links within knowledge and unity within themselves through an interactionist approach, with a clearly set-down curriculum that has tended to lead to a more formally structured approach. Froebel moved away from a set curriculum, as he was shocked by the rigidity that accompanied this way of working.

4 Children learn best when they are given appropriate responsibility, allowed to experiment, make errors, decisions and choices, and are respected as autonomous learners

Froebel, Montessori and Steiner agreed that children are self-motivating. There is no need for adults to find ways of motivating them. They do not use stars or any kind of reward system that is of the extrinsic sort. This is because extrinsic rewards cut across the child's self-motivation. The reward is intrinsic. It lies in being able to do something that could not be done before, or in knowing someone is comforted because of an act of kindness.

Froebel made the distinction between play and work. Play is what children are involved in when they initiate the task, and work is what they do when they fulfil a task required by an adult. If the child is required to work rather than to play, he or she follows a task presented to him by another, and does not reveal his or her own creativeness and inclinations but those of another.

The skill of the adult educator is in encouraging or in cooperating in the child's play, led by the initiative of the child, as a partner who shares the process. The adult may intervene sensitively (not interfere) when appropriate, so that the child is not dominated by the adult, but equally is not left to flounder.

Adults can support and extend children's play. There are moments when children do not require help and moments when they do. The skill of the adult, in Froebel's view, lies in knowing how and when to intervene. Through play, children can actively manipulate, rearrange, act on and reflect on their learning. Adults reflect through discussion, through literature, through writing and meditation. Children reflect through acting out past experiences, or preparing for them. Play helps them to grasp and try out their learning in concrete ways.

So Froebel, through his attitude to play, can be seen to value child-initiated and child-directed activity. He did not stress play as the only aspect of self-directed, self-motivated activity. He also emphasised the arts, natural science, mathematics and all the areas of knowledge in the curriculum. He saw these as another mechanism through which children would make 'the inner outer and the outer inner'. As seen in principles 2 and 3 above, processes in the child's development, and encounters with different areas of knowledge, emphasise and affect the child's ability to initiate and self-direct.

Montessori also stressed intrinsic motivation and the self-directed child initiative that results. Her 'favourable environment' was designed to encourage self-chosen tasks, but these were limited to choosing tasks to which the child had previously been introduced (such as in the exercises of practical life). In Montessori's approach, self-direction is encouraged by 'real' tasks, or apparatus that is based on Montessori's observation of children's natural concerns; for example, the way children love to put objects into rows or to build towers. However, Montessori did not value play. She saw it as an insult to the child. 'If I were persuaded that children need to play, I would provide the proper apparatus, but I am not so persuaded' (Kilpatrick, 1915: 42). She felt that children search for a real life. Rather than toys, Montessori argues:

> We must give the child an environment that he can utilise by himself: and a little wash-stand of his own, some small chairs, a bureau with drawers he can open, objects of common use that he can operate, a small bed in which he can sleep at night under an attractive blanket he can fold and spread by himself.

(Montessori, 1975: 116)

Her exercises of practical life were geared towards real household tasks, and children work their way through these only if they have been introduced to them. Only then do they have freedom of choice.

> To take certain objects and to present them in a certain fashion to the child, and then to leave the child alone with them and not to interfere.
>
> (Montessori, 1949: 253)

Her materials offered children choices of a different nature, within a prescribed sequence. For Montessori, children need a prepared environment in which the complicated world is simplified by means of a set sequence for the children to move through, with the tranquillity that develops concentration. The highest moment is the silence that attends the 'polarisation of the attention', when the child is so absorbed that he or she is not in communication with others. Self-motivation is fed most by isolating children from the world, and its height is reached by their choosing to isolate themselves within the prepared environment that was so designed that they may be enabled and free to do so (Bruce, 1976).

Steiner dealt with self-directed activity differently. He describes how during the early years, the child lives mainly in the 'will' element, where the child learns through doing, through movement and activity. The head is the physical base for thinking, the rhythmical system (breathing and circulation) is the centre for the feeling life, and the limbs provide the physical means for expressing the will.

During the period up to seven years of age, teachers take care to ensure that nothing is done that will weaken or otherwise compromise the child's physical constitution. Warm clothing, organic food, carefully chosen sensory experiences, and a general protective gesture towards the child's physical well-being are central features of the child's care.

The challenge for the Steiner early years/childhood teacher is 'How do I work with the unconscious will forces of the child under seven so that these forces gradually become self-directed responses?' There is an additional responsibility arising from accepting that, in early childhood,

> … the foundation is laid for the development of a strong and healthy will.
>
> (Steiner, in Oldfield, 2003: 53)

Oldfield stresses that Steiner believed children reach stages of development in the first seven years at different times. The key to the next stage is when the child actively wants to do things out of their own initiative, usually around six or seven years, when the teacher understands and begins to work with the temperament of each child.

Self-directed activity varies according to the different approaches. Froebel emphasised the value of play and language, active learning, involving choice and freedom to experiment and make errors, expressive feelings and thoughts carried out through the child's initiatives. Montessori emphasised the value of real tasks, and choice within those, and Steiner emphasised the different needs of the stages he identified. Choice comes after the will has been established. Until then imitation (copying) is emphasised. However, all three stressed intrinsic motivation, and rejected reward systems and extrinsic motivation.

> 5 Self-discipline is emphasised as the only kind of discipline worth having. Reward systems are very short term and do not work in the long term in developing moral and spiritual aspects of living. Children need their efforts to be valued and appreciated

The development of self-discipline is closely linked with intrinsic motivation, and with the need to promote it by allowing children to initiate and self-regulate tasks, activities and ideas. Self-discipline is probably one of the most important elements in life. Without it, no matter how imaginative, creative, logical or skilful a person is, there will be no development towards the completion of the work. Froebel, Montessori and Steiner all agreed that self-discipline emerged from keeping intrinsic motivation intact. This is probably the area of greatest agreement between them. In other respects, they have deep and far-reaching arguments, between friends in that their principles are shared, but the different interpretations lead to such different practices that it is sometimes hard to see why they are friends. They are all interactionists (not empiricists or nativists), but of very different kinds.

We saw how Froebel emphasised play as a means by which the child willingly sees things through to completion and an integrated whole. This sort of environment is conducive to the development of self-discipline – the strong, confident self with sufficiently high self-esteem not to be distracted from fulfilling an objective or working towards ideals. Froebel (1887: 131) said: 'The faith and trust, the hope and anticipation with which the child enters school accomplishes everything.'

The early childhood practitioner must not destroy this, but a dialogue with and respect for the child will help self-discipline emerge – a discipline that is an inner influence rather than an external force. The partnership element of the relationship between adult and child was stressed. The adult helps the child to articulate and understand events in which he or she has participated through language, play and activities. Inner influence rather than external force is the key to the emergence of self-discipline. Froebel would shudder to see any kind of extrinsic reward.

At the centre of Froebel's approach to discipline was his belief that the child's intrinsic motivation should not be damaged. This is encouraged by his belief that humans are basically good. He rejected the notion of original sin. He said:

… the only and infallible remedy for counteracting any shortcoming and even wickedness is to find the originally good source, the originally good side of the human being that has been repressed, disturbed, or misled into the shortcoming, and then to foster, build up, and properly guide this good side. Thus the shortcoming will at last disappear, although it may involve a hard struggle against habit, but not against original depravity in man.

(Froebel, 1887: 121–122)

In developing self-discipline in the child, Froebel placed emphasis on discussion between the adult and the child in bringing to light this good tendency. Discussion helps the child to analyse and reflect, to come to an understanding of the implications of actions and so to work out a solution to problems. This has much resonance with the work of REPEY (Researching Effective Pedagogy in the Early Years) on 'shared sustained conversations' and the project approach of Reggio Emilia.

Froebel emphasised mutual respect, and a truly reciprocal partnership between child and adult is central to his philosophy. Froebel's attitude to self-discipline leads towards an informally structured interactionist curriculum. Children may not harm others, or equipment.

Montessori also asserted the importance of self-discipline. She did so by stressing the child's need for protection from the over-dominating adult in a prepared environment. If a child acts in a way that is regarded as unacceptable, he or she is asked to sit and watch the others at work. The child who is separated from the 'overdirective, cacophonic' inputs of adults

needs rest and a peaceful sameness in order to construct his inner life: yet, instead, we disturb him with our continual, brutal interruptions. We hurl a quantity of disordered impressions at him that are often sustained with such rapidity that he has not time to absorb them. Then the child cries in the same way that he would if he were hungry or had eaten too much and was feeling the first signs of digestive disturbance.

(Montessori, 1975: 127)

There are limits to self-discipline. Montessori (1912: 87) said: 'The liberty of the child should have as its limit the collective interest.' The disciplining of the child is approached by isolating the child who transgresses, so that he/she can experience the tranquillity of the favourable environment by observing other children:

This isolation succeeds in calming the mind: from this position he could see the entire assembly of his companions, and the way in which they carried on their work was an object lesson much more efficacious than any words of the teacher could possibly have been.

(Montessori, 1912: 87)

Froebel and Montessori encouraged self-discipline in different ways. Froebel stressed play and discourse with adults and other children, so that the child begins to think through the consequences of his or her actions, and how these have affected others and self. Montessori stressed tranquillity in the 'favourable environment' and observing others. This is more akin to the modern use of the 'time-out chair'. The idea here is that the child will absorb through imitation (copying) the good behaviour of others. However, both Froebel and Montessori agreed that self-discipline was of central importance in the development of the child.

Steiner also asserted the importance of self-discipline. Like Froebel and Montessori, he saw it as emerging from allowing the child's natural willingness to learn, to initiate, and to create an ability to self-regulate during development. He emphasised the need to have a broad understanding of the world that will awaken human potential. Like Froebel, he stressed the community as a powerful influence in the development of self-discipline.

In a Steiner education the aim is to help each person find his or her right place in life, to fulfil his or her destiny. Self-discipline is a part of this. In contrast to Froebel's emphasis on conversation and language, in the Steiner approach discussion is not introduced until much later. In this respect, Steiner and Montessori are closer to each other. They saw the child as absorbing the environment in the early years. Discussion of the cause and effects of behaviours and actions is not seen as a mechanism through which children begin to reflect on situations in the development of self-discipline.

Steiner's children first develop through the atmosphere created by the parent/teacher in the first seven years. Then their temperament is supported, in the middle years, by the authority of the teacher who extends them further – for example, with stories, songs and history. Only later, in adolescence, does discussion relating to ideas and knowledge dominate the approach to self-discipline.

Froebel and Steiner emphasised the importance of the community of adults and children in the development of self-discipline. Froebel stressed the need for discourse as an aspect of this. In contrast, Montessori required a tranquil setting, free from over-dominant adults or children who cut across the self-disciplined work of another child. Steiner and Montessori stressed the way in which children imitate their surroundings, and constructed prescribed environments in which to set children where they can be protected from damaging external influences and the outside world. Froebel's children are in the real world from the beginning of their lives.

6 There are times when children are especially able to learn particular things

The end of the previous section leads to the need for some consideration of stage theory in the philosophies of Froebel, Montessori and Steiner. Both Montessori and Steiner prescribed set procedures to deal with each stage in the child's development. In other words, stages in the child are closely linked with curriculum content and the environment in which the child is set. In Froebel's later philosophy, curriculum content and the child's environment are not prescribed.

Froebel's belief 'At every stage be that stage' summarises his view. He designed the Gifts and Occupations to make use of each stage in development. For example, the soft sphere is the first Gift; the wooden sphere, cylinder and cube the second; while the Occupations include paper-folding, plaiting, cutting and pricking paper, working with clay, woodwork, sewing, drawing and stick-laying.

The message he gave was to allow children fully to experience within the level at which they are functioning, rather than to attempt to accelerate them on to the next stage. He argued for activities that are broad (rather than narrow and designed only to reach the next step in the hierarchy of knowledge as quickly as possible). The skill of the adult lies in observing the child and, acting in the light of observations, extending at that level (Bruce, 1978, 1984, 1987).

'At every stage be that stage' was for Froebel optimised by paying attention to physical activity, aesthetic knowledge (feelings) and scientific knowledge (thought). In this way the child fully experiences each stage across interconnected and linked forms. This links with Froebel's view that every stage exists in its own right. Speedy acceleration towards adulthood cuts across breadth and depth of knowledge and experience. A richly developed person is more likely to emerge if children are encouraged fully to experience the stage at which they are.

Montessori's notion of the 'sensitive period' (which she took from the Dutch biologist Hugo de Vries) is probably her most important contribution to the education of young children (Bruce, 1976; Bruce et al., 1995). Sensitive periods occur when 'an irresistible impulse urges the organism to select only certain elements in its environment, and for a definite, limited time' (Montessori, 1949). She was very specific about the way these sensitive periods should be dealt with, and here she parts company with Froebel. She lays down precisely, in what she called her scientific method, how her didactic materials, exercises of practical life and potters' arts should be used to get the most out of such periods. They allow for the practising of maturing skills during sensitive periods and they contrast with Froebel's more open-ended approach. Children work through the hierarchy according to prescribed methods, and are allowed choice only when they demonstrate they can follow these.

Steiner also saw certain stages in development as particularly receptive and requiring certain attention; for example, at 12 years old Steiner believes it is right for children to start physics, chemistry and mechanics. Steiner was more like Montessori in his reaction to stages of development, as he set down precisely what was appropriate in his method.

Although there has been a tendency to interpret Montessori's approach in a prescriptive way in the training colleges, in fact it is only in the use of Seguin's 'Three Period Lesson' that her instructions are specific. Barbara Isaacs (personal communication, 2004) points out that, in *The Discovery of the Child* (1948), Montessori discusses 'the limitations of prescribed presentation, as she is aware of the dangers in limiting the child's exploration and self-learning'. Froebel was less precise about what ought to be done during sensitive periods, in terms of the exact knowledge children should meet or experiences they should encounter. His concern was for adults to recognise stages of order through observing a child carefully, and work out their own ways of acting upon their insights. At one stage he began setting out more specific instructions, but later moved away from this more curriculum-based and adult-focused approach to his earlier child-focused work. This was probably because he found that adults used his Gifts and Occupations too narrowly (Liebschner, 1991, 1992). Montessori and Steiner prescribed specific action that left the adult with less choice.

These different views of how to build on the stages or sensitive periods led to important practical differences in approach that are still seen today. Froebel's view led to an indirectly structured approach. This relied heavily on sound initial training and later good-quality in-service training for teachers, studying child development and acquiring knowledge of the subject to be taught. His is an open system, with incompleteness (an unfinished state) an important ingredient for ensuring development – with great responsibility devolving upon the practitioner. In contrast, Montessori and Steiner led to a more internally, though still indirectly, structured approach, which was a complete system in itself. This carries the danger of rigid and ossified practice.

Froebel, Montessori and Steiner all believed that there are definite stages in development that require appropriate and sensitive handling. They all asserted that each stage is important in its own right and should not be accelerated, but enriched at that level instead. The difference lies in that Froebel did not prescribe how children are taken through each stage, so that this is an approach that is more open to developing theories and research findings. But it also gives a framework for the interpretation of theory and research, so that it does not sway with every new fashion and fad in education.

7 What children can do (rather than what they cannot do) is the starting point for a child's learning

The idea of starting with what children can do, rather than with what they cannot do, is common to Froebel, Montessori and Steiner. This, like their thinking on intrinsic reward, is an area on which they agree fully, but as always, this is in principle rather than in practice. Froebel's belief in this principle is encapsulated in one of his most famous remarks: 'Begin where the learner is, not where the learner ought to be.' For Froebel, play alerts the adult to what the child is able to do and what is needed in order both to support and, very importantly, to extend learning at that stage. He saw play as a mediating factor between the knowledge the child is acquiring, be it aesthetic, humanistic or scientific, and the natural and spiritual development within the child.

Like Froebel, Montessori stressed observing children in order to see what they can do, and to build on this. Her approach was based on the observations she made of children, many of them with special needs. These observations may account for the particular emphasis her method placed on action and the lack of emphasis on imagination and language. She developed didactic materials, exercises of practical life and graded sequences to exploit what the child could do, and to help each child develop at his or her own pace in carefully spaced steps. Her Three-Part Language lesson demonstrates her desire to build on success, rather than to emphasise weakness. At the point of failure, the sequence is stopped.

> Then in order to teach the colours, she says, showing him the red, 'This is the red', raising her voice a little and pronouncing the word 'red' slowly and clearly; then showing him the other colour, 'This is blue.' In order to make sure that the child has understood, she says to him, 'Give me the red, give me the blue.' Let us suppose that the child, following the last direction, made a mistake. The teacher does not repeat, and she does not insist: she smiles, gives the child a friendly caress, and takes away the colours.
>
> (Montessori, 1912: 109)

In order to assess the point in the sequences at which the child has arrived, and to use the materials or sequences properly, the directress must be a proficient observer of children. Froebel and Montessori also stressed the importance of observing children and building on what they can do, in order to make the most use of each stage of development.

Steiner also subscribed to this view. In the early years (up to seven years of age), the will is dominant as the child works actively in the limbs. Emphasis is placed on physical activity. Steiner's belief in reincarnation led him to suggest that the adult needs to observe the child and work at providing a suitable environment that provides for the needs of each child at their particular stage of development. In this way the environment can be structured for the teacher to build on the child's strengths by using what the child can do; it encourages physical activity (baking, painting, planting a garden, for example) and allows for imitation as the child absorbs his or her surroundings. The aim is to go with the child's abilities, not against them.

In different ways, Froebel, Montessori and Steiner emphasised what the child can do now, in the present. All three asserted the importance of building on strength and what the child can do, because this does not damage the intrinsic motivation or developing self-discipline of the child.

Through careful observation, based on knowledge of the stages of child development, the adult can work with the child rather than against what is natural. The stages of knowledge of both Steiner and Montessori are based on the original framing of the methods associated with their approach. Froebelian stages have linked with current theory and research, but kept the essence of active physical and sensory learning, movement, communication and language being important, expression of ideas, thoughts and feelings, the symbolic life of the child becoming central, which are part of the original stages Froebel emphasised.

8 Diverse kinds of symbolic behaviour develop and emerge when learning environments conducive to this are created at home, in early childhood settings, indoors and outdoors

The inner life of the child was deeply valued by Froebel, Montessori and Steiner. It featured especially in children's imagination, creativity, symbolic functioning and language. Froebel stressed that children need help in absorbing and transforming knowledge into clear ideas, feelings and knowledge. He emphasised physical knowledge, aesthetic knowledge and scientific knowledge, and helped children to develop these through the Mother Songs (Froebel, 1878), Gifts, Occupations and Movement Games (Liebschner, 1991, 1992), and direct experience of nature (for example in gardening). He saw conversations as an important part of this process. He stressed play as an integrating mechanism (Froebel, 1887: 55). Children also need to share these learning experiences, and to use the knowledge they have 'processed' and 'transformed'. The activities mentioned also have this possibility. Children use clay, draw and paint, fold paper (the Occupations), use wooden blocks (bricks), the Gifts, and work in the garden. Froebel aimed 'to make the outer inner and the inner outer' through a wide range of experiences.

He emphasised that play, the imagination and the ability of the mind could make the 'inner outer', to transform knowledge, 'to associate facts into principles'. He stressed the importance of images through the Mother Songs (Froebel, 1878) and through interacting with nature. He says that the child needs help in sharing his or her knowledge through using paint, clay, music, dance, drama, written work, conversation and mathematics, and in many other ways. The inner life of the child is fed through imagery, imitation (in the sense of reconstruction and transformation by the child, rather than passive copying), and the child's developing ability in language and non-verbal representation (the symbolic mechanisms) (see Bruce et al., 1995). Physical activity, language, the arts and natural sciences are all of critical importance in Froebel's approach. They feed different aspects of the transformation between inner and outer.

One of the greatest contributions to early childhood education that Froebel made was in his thinking about the symbolic life of the child, and the importance of play, the arts, sciences and humanities in relation to the child becoming both a symbol user and a symbol maker. This is further explored in Chapters 5, 6 and 7.

Montessori's approach to symbolic development is totally different to that of Froebel. For example, she uses Seguin's three-period vocabulary lesson as the basis of her approach to language work. She drew on Seguin's work because he had achieved remarkable results with children with learning difficulties, and she had also begun her work in education with mentally disabled children (Lane, 1977). Her use of Seguin's three-period vocabulary lesson, which involved giving vocabulary that is first imitated by the child, then spontaneously produced by the child, does not emphasise the transformational aspect of the inner life of the child in the way that Froebel does. For Montessori, knowledge, as it stands, is absorbed and used. For Froebel, knowledge is absorbed, but transformed in the process and, after acquisition, stored in the imagination. For Montessori, tranquillity is the key to the inner life. She describes her lesson with the seriated cylinders:

> These lessons may appear strange, because they are carried out in almost complete silence, while one thinks in general that a lesson signifies an oral recitation, almost a tiny lecture. The teacher never encourages this tranquillity with words, but with her own quiet sureness. Thus, we can say that our own 'tranquillity lessons' are symbolic of our method.
>
> (1975: 137)

The child absorbs the teacher's tranquillity. It is the practitioner's skilled contribution to the tranquillity in the 'favourable environment' that is of fundamental support to the child's self-motivation and the development of the will and subsequent inner life that helps the child to directly absorb what is before him or her. The seriated cylinders are copied within the child, and so the outer becomes inner. Language does not feed the inner life in the way that it does for Froebel. Imitation is copy rather than reconstruction.

Steiner, on the other hand, like Froebel, stressed the inner life as the child transforms experiences through the imagination, but not during the initial stages of childhood. In the early years (the first seven years when the will is becoming established), the Grimms' fairy stories are sometimes told (among other stories) and these present wisdom in picture form, giving a pictorial understanding of the world and developing the moral sense. Most important, according to Janni Nicol (personal communication, 2004), is the use of imitation of the teacher who provides a loving moral example for the child.

In approaching the first seven years, Steiner is in some respects closer to Montessori than to Froebel. The emphasis is on imitation as absorbing or copying, rather than Froebel's emphasis on reconstruction. Children speak, sing, model, paint, perform household duties (including gardening), absorbing what surrounds them like blotting paper. Imagination is stressed through fairy stories (wisdom in picture form), but a child is seen to drink in and absorb the environment without at first much transformation.

The Steinerian view is that the child needs sensory protection from the world outside the early childhood setting (for instance, the wrong colour scheme in rooms, inappropriate toys or TV and electronic media or books), and this continues to some extent into middle childhood. In other words, the emphasis in the first two periods of life is on the outer surroundings becoming internalised through absorbing that which surrounds the child. It is not until the last period that independent thinking is considered to emerge, and the inner transforms and uses what has been absorbed.

The inner life of the child is directly helped through graded sequences and experiences in a prepared environment by Montessori's method. Steiner also created a community where the child meets carefully selected experiences, led directly by the adult. Both offer direct formally structured curricula. For Froebel, the curriculum was informally structured. This is a major difference between Froebel and the other two pioneers.

The adult, using the tools of the child's burgeoning symbolic processes – the imagination, language, objects, people, places and events – works informally with the child, often indirectly. The adult still controls and manipulates the situation, but less tangibly. Everything provided in the learning environment indoors and outdoors in the garden is there for a reason, but the Froebelian approach is more open ended in the way children use what is offered, and choose to explore and experiment.

Froebel, Montessori and Steiner all stressed the inner life of the child. Steiner and Montessori are alike in their approach to the early years of education in that they stressed children's ability to absorb into themselves their experiences of their surroundings. In the later years, Steiner and Froebel throughout the child's development emphasised the child's ability to transform experiences as they are taken in so that they fit with previous learning, or cause modification in what has previously been learned. For all three, the inner life is one of the most important aspects of the child's development, but there are deep differences in the way this is carried out in practice.

9 Relationships with other people (both adults and children) are of central importance in a child's life, influencing emotional and social well-being

Froebel saw the mother as the first educator in the child's life – a revolutionary view at a time when only men were seen as capable of teaching children. The adult is a partner in the child's learning, not a threat to it. First the adults in the family, then the teacher, help and guide the child into the wider community. Through play, children manipulate, reflect, extend and experiment with their learning about social relationships, feelings and ideas. The adult is the child's helper, through conversation and provision of appropriate materials, the arbitrator in quarrels and the orchestrator of the child's learning with other children and adults, objects, places and events. At different times children have different needs in terms of social interaction. Sometimes the adult leads and the child follows, sometimes the reverse.

The community was important in a Froebelian kindergarten. The children would dance and sing in the village square in the early kindergartens, and events and significant moments were shared, with the kindergarten at the heart of these. The kindergarten was not separate from the wider word, but part of it.

Similarly, the child interacts with other children. At times children need to be alone, at times together. Other children are an essential part of Froebel's philosophy. They need to play together, to learn to negotiate, lead, follow, learn about the results of quarrels, to experience making music and to dance as a group.

Montessori saw adults, including parents, as a threat to the child's freedom, in the sense that they need to be, according to Barbara Isaacs (personal communication, 2004), 'a controlling influence in the child's life and so were other children. Her approach enabled the child to escape into independence, concentration and tranquillity. She advocates adults taking responsibility for their actions and to respect and trust the child's inner motivation and driving force.' She points out that in *The Discovery of the Child* (1948), in the chapter on 'Walking on the line', Montessori writes about the importance of letting children resolve their own conflicts rather than intervening.

The practitioner organises the prepared environment so that at times the child can do things alone without help. However, Barbara Isaacs (personal communication, 2004) shows how in the chapter on 'Cohesion of the social unit', in her book, *The Absorbent Mind* (1949), Montessori writes about the importance of allowing the child's natural interest in other children to foster social awareness in the group.

Froebel, Steiner and Montessori felt mixed age groups of children encourage social development. Montessori designed the more advanced materials in the sensorial areas to encourage shared use and recognise the child's growing ability to think from other people's points of view.

Steiner and Montessori in different ways, like Froebel, emphasised the adult, peers and family. Montessori saw the child as guiding not simply him or herself, but also the practitioner, towards self-mastery in life. Barbara Isaacs suggests that Montessori included in this both social interactions and growing awareness of the group. Although the 'favourable environment' was tranquil, this does not mean there was silence in it. Children are free to speak, although there is less emphasis on language and discussion than in the Froebelian approach.

For Steiner the emphasis on the adult, other children and family was especially important initially, when the child absorbs the moral atmosphere projected by the family and school: 'What is of the very greatest importance is what kind of men we are, what impressions the child receives through us, whether it can imitate us' (Steiner, 1926: 22). Social interaction generally is greatly encouraged; for example, through emphasis on free, imaginative child-led play, self-initiated creativity, language and caring for each other.

Of the three approaches, Montessori's and Steiner's are found to be formally and directly structured curricula, while Froebel's is informally and indirectly structured. For all its intangibility, the informally structured curriculum has stood the test of time to a remarkable extent; it influenced key curriculum framework documents in the four countries of the UK and continues to do so.

This more open-ended Froebelian interpretation of the ten principles has proved particularly receptive to the findings of later educationalists, especially those working from the interactionist standpoint. The next chapter looks at how four classic theorists have supported the ten principles and refined their practical implementation – in short, the early childhood traditions reasserted and extended.

3

Ten principles in a modern context

In this chapter, classic theories and recent supporting evidence demonstrate that the ten early childhood principles discussed in the previous chapter remain important for the early childhood practitioner, revisited so that the principles resonate with the modern lenses through which practice is viewed and developed. This leads to increased sophistication in early childhood practice through a better understanding of the ubiquities that remain at the heart of early childhood practice in an increasingly diverse and complex world.

Jean Piaget (1896–1980), Lev Vygotsky (1896–1934), Mia Kellmer Pringle (1920–1983) and Jerome Bruner (1915–), each in different ways, help us to think about our work today. Their areas of agreement, disagreement, and where they can never agree or where their disagreements can be reconciled, are deeply useful for practitioners now. Their contributions have been, and in Bruner's case still are, of the classic and lasting kind.

It is important to bear in mind socio-cultural influences on theorists. Any theory arises out of the social context in which that theory is formulated. The culture, the people who live with and work with the theorists, will have a huge impact on how ideas are developed (Bruce, 1997a).

In the previous chapter, it was emphasised that Froebel, Montessori and Steiner, although innovative and original, were nevertheless thinking according to the influences of the historical and cultural context in which they lived. It is the mark of great thinkers that they can readjust to changing times without losing the essentials of their work. It is therefore likely that if they were to return in the next millennium, they would significantly change their terminology and reflect, modify and extend their theories (Moyles, 2005). Because Froebel did not set his philosophy in any specific method, his thinking is more easily open to developments of this kind.

The context for Jerome Bruner in the USA is an entirely different one to that of Europe, where Piaget and Kellmer Pringle lived. On the other hand, the USA, UK and Switzerland have capitalism in common, but this contrasts with the Marxist context in which Vygotsky grew up. Not only this, but Piaget was an only child, while Vygotsky was one of several children in a large family. It then seems obvious why Piaget focused on the actively exploring, autonomous learning child, while Vygotsky proposed that all higher learning develops out of social relationships.

Mia Kellmer Pringle, remembered for her pioneer work as Director of the UK National Children's Bureau in the late 1960s, lost much of her close family in Nazi concentration camps. It is understandable that she emphasised children's fundamental needs, building on the work of Susan Isaacs and Maslow's hierarchy of needs. Her work embraces the development of the whole child in the family.

The work of these important thinkers resonates with the bedrock principles of traditional early childhood practice in ways that help us to move forward. Although the work of each could be used to illustrate each and every principle, this would become another book. Instead, selected examples from each thinker have been used to make links with some of the principles.

1 The best way to prepare children for their adult life is to give them what they need as children

Bruner's thinking has moved forward since he formulated the notion of the spiral curriculum (1977). However, it remains very useful in helping practitioners to make links between what is appropriate and relevant to the child in the here and now, and how this needs to have nesting within it the emergent essentials of later more complex, abstract and sophisticated knowledge. In Chapter 1, Damasio's biological 'nesting principle' was introduced. Bruner's spiral curriculum offers us a socio-cultural nesting principle, which intertwines powerfully with biology.

> Learning should not only take us somewhere; it should allow us later to go further more easily.
>
> (Bruner, 1977: 17)

Finger painting is an activity in which young children often participate in at schools, day nurseries, playgroups and sometimes at home. It involves children in transforming coloured powder into coloured sludge. Transformations of materials from powder to solid are central to the later study of science, particularly chemistry. In this way, it is possible to help very young children to learn the essentials of chemistry in ways appropriate for them. Children are fascinated by whether this is a reversible transformation. Can this sludge be turned back into powder again?

The spiral curriculum enables the early childhood practitioner to match the child's development with areas of learning, such as knowledge and understanding of the world.

> Any subject can be taught to any child at any age in some form that is honest.
>
> (Bruner, 1977: ix)

In the same way, the baby in the high chair, who drops custard on the floor and watches it splat, and then crumbles biscuit crumbs over the edge, watching them fall, is experiencing in an emergent way the impact of gravity and so is learning physics, if the adult comments on what the baby is looking at: 'Did it go zoom – splat on the floor?'

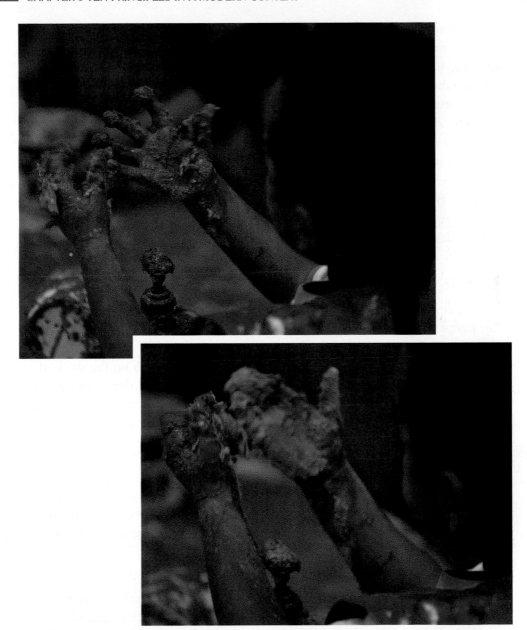

Figure 3.1: The science in finger painting – can the sludge be transformed back into powder paint?

Bruner suggests that practitioners should consider whether something contains possibilities for future learning in some simple form. If not, it can be rejected as 'clutter'. Bruner has consistently emphasised how practitioners need to be sure they are preparing children for later learning and knowledge.

Across the years, he has increasingly emphasised the role of the adult and the socio-cultural aspects of learning. However, it is important to remember, when he asserts that adults need to act as scaffolding, which, he suggests, supports children in moving from where they are now to where adults want to take them, that scaffolding is external to the child. We need to be clear that this is different from a situation where the adult goes with the child and helps them to learn more about what interests and fascinates them, as Anna Freud advocates (see Bruce, 2004).

Bruner's famous paper (Bruner *et al.*, 1976) emphasises the adult's need to look at what the child's 'incipient intention' seems to be, and to lead the child from that to the adult's learning intention for the child.

The differences are subtle and sophisticated, and the balance between the two is delicate. Both are important, but knowing which to use when requires skill.

2 Children are whole people who have feelings, ideas, a sense of embodied self and relationships with others, and who need to be physically, mentally, morally and spiritually healthy

In later chapters we shall look at how the early relationships of children with other people who matter to them (usually family and carers) contribute to the way they are equipped to develop later in life.

Kellmer Pringle's thinking (1974 (second edition, 1980)) built on the work of Maslow (1962) and Susan Isaacs in the 1930s. Isaacs emphasised that primary needs of nourishment, shelter and clothing are necessary for survival, but that secondary needs of love, security, new experiences, praise and recognition, and taking responsibility are also of fundamental importance as children develop and learn.

Feelings and emotions

This links with the recent work in neuroscience on the development of feelings and emotions. Antonio Damasio (2004) makes a distinction between emotions and feelings, which helps us in our work with children. He argues that emotions lead to feelings.

* Emotions are public. They show in our actions, facial expressions, body temperature, movements and voice. They show in our hormonal and electro-physical wave patterns. They are not hidden. They cause physical reactions in our bodies.
* Feelings are not public. They are hidden (like mental images) and they are, he says, our most private property.

Emotions (Damasio, 2004: 30) developed in evolution to promote survival.
Emotions help us to:

* find sources of energy we need to respond to situations;
* transform energy;
* maintain chemical balance;
* maintain our bodies against wear and tear;
* fend off disease and injury.

Damasio has developed the 'nesting principle'. This means that the simple nests
within the complex. The simple emotions of joy, sorrow, fear, pride, shame,
sympathy, disgust, anger arise from reflexes, immune responses, metabolic
balances, pain and pleasure drives, all incorporated (nested) in the machinery of
emotions proper.

Damasio argues that some of these emotions can be used in maladaptive ways
in modern life. It is no longer useful, or appropriate, to greet those who are
different with aggression or withdrawal, seeing them as a risk or danger. We now
think of this as discriminatory (see Chapter 10).

These primary emotions nest within the social emotions we begin to develop,
such as sympathy, empathy, love, embarrassment, shame, guilt, humiliation, pride,
jealousy, envy, gratitude, admiration, indignation and contempt.

> The nesting of the simple within the complex ensures that the regulatory
> purpose remains present in the higher echelons of the chain.
>
> (Damasio, 2004: 49)

> Humans have developed will-power to override the tyrannical automaticity
> and mindlessness of the emotional machinery.
>
> (Damasio, 2004: 52)

Overall, emotions help us to 'read' ourselves, other people and situations, and
to respond accordingly and adaptively. When we feel sad, the ability to think is
decreased. When we have well-being, the ability to think is increased.

Attachment and emotional well-being

From a different perspective, the psycho-dynamically trained Sue Gerhardt
(2004) has attempted to make links with her expertise and that of insights gained
from the neurosciences. She emphasises the role of the adult in responding to
the early emotions of babies and children, arguing that 'our minds emerge and
our emotions become organised through engagement with other minds, not in
isolation' (Gerhardt, 2004: 15). Like Damasio, she gives a major place to non-
verbal communication through tone of voice, warm, affectionate touch, facial

expression and movement. 'Early emotion is very much about pushing people away or drawing them closer' (Gerhardt, 2004: 19).

She gives a powerful example of how to calm a baby:

… by mirroring a baby's state with him (her), engaging him with a loud mirroring voice. Gradually leading the way towards calm by toning her voice down, and taking him with her to a calmer state.

(Gerhardt, 2004: 23)

This takes the baby back to their comfort zone again, by tuning in to the baby's emotional state and acting appropriately in the light of this.

Good relationships, she argues (2004: 25), depend on finding a reasonable balance between being able to track your own feelings at the same time as you track other people's. Children who are helped to recognise how they feel, and to identify this so that they express how they feel appropriately, are more easily helped to thoughtfully reflect. Children develop well if they are able to tune in to and read how they feel, and coordinate that with how others feel. David Goleman (1996) calls this emotional intelligence. It involves:

* empathising and tuning in to others;
* vicariously experiencing what they experience;
* inferring someone else's feelings and thoughts;
* deciding what it is socially acceptable and appropriate to do.

Developing self-discipline, developing thoughtful feelings

Emotions play an important part in self-regulation, as we shall see in later chapters. They help us to respond to situations and people, enabling us to reflect and guiding what we do. They help us to have what we might call thoughtful feelings, rather than to be overwhelmed by raw emotions, which stem the flow of information within us in unhelpful and damaging ways.

Babies and young children depend on adults to help them manage stressful situations. They need physical comfort, warmth and affection from people who matter to them. Good attachment, a concept pioneered by John Bowlby, gives babies a good start in this.

Figure 3.2: The older child holds back her feelings when the younger child draws on her drawing (B), but she has developed strategies to protect her drawing (C), and to help the younger child to understand that this is not an acceptable thing to do.

The whole child and multi-agency work

Nutrition, outdoor play, appropriate clothing and rest all contribute to the physical health of children. The five strands of the Children Act (2005) all emphasise the whole child in a spirit of diversity and inclusion. They are to:

* be healthy;
* stay safe;
* achieve and enjoy;
* make a positive contribution;
* experience economic well-being.

3 Areas of learning involving the humanities, arts and sciences cannot be separated; young children learn in an integrated way and not in neat, tidy compartments

Kellmer Pringle emphasises that the child who is loved may or may not enjoy a deep sense of security and well-being. A child may be praised, but may not be given recognition (Kohn, 1993). Appreciation and recognition should link with every other aspect of the child's needs.

Six-year-old **NIKOLAI** was working with a student teacher who praised every step in his model-making. After a while, Nikolai looked up, and said, 'Why do you keep saying, "good"?' In this example, praise was given in isolation from any real achievement or effort.

DAISY is learning to crawl. She keeps going backwards instead of forwards, and is finding this frustrating. She sinks on her stomach on the floor, and then has another go; this time she pushes her knee on the floor and looks amazed as she edges forwards. The childminder, Sue, says, 'Oh well done Daisy! What a good push!' Daisy smiles and tries again.

Being acknowledged and affirmed is important for young children.

Piaget's view of human development as a matrix or network emphasises the interconnectedness of the growth and knowledge of understanding feelings and relationships with the development of thinking. He identified connected networks:

* logical–mathematical;
* social–temporal;
* physical;
* symbolic representation;
* the impossibility of separating thinking, feelings and relationships.

He and Kellmer Pringle express the wholeness of learning in different ways, but with the same messages for practitioners.

Figure 3.3: The boy is encouraged to experiment, make errors and choices, and is respected as an autonomous learner.

4 Children learn best when they are given appropriate responsibility, allowed to experiment, make errors, decisions and choices, and are respected as autonomous learners

Kellmer Pringle emphasises that the will to learn has its roots in the quality of relationships the child experiences, especially in early life. More recently, attention has turned to the importance of dispositions towards learning (Katz, 1993; Carr, 1999, 2001) and the importance of well-being (Laevers, 1994; Pascal and Bertram, 1997).

The introduction of the early childhood curriculum frameworks in the four countries of the UK supports the embedding of learning environments indoors and outdoors that are conducive to encouraging autonomous learning.

In a different way, Piaget encourages self-regulation in learning, through the process of equilibration. This has two aspects:

1. assimilation – children absorb experiences into what they already know;
2. accommodation – children need to change and adjust what they know in order to take in something that does not fit.

> Two-year-old **ROBERT** had established that wheels are round. This view had been well-assimilated through a variety of experiences, but he was then confronted with a long toy caterpillar with square wheels, which moved along when pulled by a string. This was surprising and novel, and he had to adjust his thinking to take this in (accommodation). He was taking responsibility for his learning, making choices and decisions.

Through Piaget's concept of self-regulation in learning (which continues through life), children experience a range of feelings. Recognising what is familiar, and repeating what is known and comfortable, bring enjoyment and the deep pleasure of play and humour, or the boredom that comes when familiarity brings the need to find new things to do.

Accommodation brings with it surprise, fascination of the new, anger that something does not fit previous knowledge, struggle and frustration. Intrinsic motivation and autonomy of learning are valued in different ways by both Kellmer Pringle and Piaget. There are strong resonances here with the writings of Damasio, Gerhardt and Goleman, who also give a central place to the role of the adult in supporting children to be autonomous learners. It is important to make connections across different disciplines and theories if we are to find the cross-cultural ubiquities that help us to understand how to help children develop and learn.

Balancing child-initiated and adult-led learning

Throughout the literature the issues surrounding the delicacy of balance between child-initiated learning and adult-led learning are a recurring theme.

There is a difference between adults intervening to help children, and adults interfering. There is also a difference between leaving children to do as they like and helping children to take initiative, make choices and decisions, learn from errors and be autonomous learners. Vygotsky's proposal was that there are zones of actual, potential and future development.

Figure 3.4: The adult is sitting with the child, who watches as she writes down the story. This is called scribing for the child.

Vygotsky's zone of actual development – the fruits of development

The zone of actual development (Vygotsky, 1978: 86) shows the already matured structures, which he calls the 'fruits of development'. They show what the child can do alone and without help.

The zone of proximal or potential development – the buds of development

This shows structures that are still in the process of maturing, 'functions that will mature tomorrow but are currently in an embryonic state' (Vygotsky, 1978: 86). He sees these as the 'buds of development'. They show what the child can manage to do only with help from another more advanced child, or an adult. The child is therefore on the edge of his or her capabilities, and this is why support is needed.

The zone of future development

This is what the child will be able to do alone and without help at a later point of development.

Four-year-old **HANNAH** wanted to choreograph a dance and share it with her teacher, for whom it was intended as a present. Her teacher, Charlotte, had been away for a few days. Hannah has an idea that the dance will be called 'Looking for Charlotte', but she needs to talk to an adult (her mother) about it. She needs someone to listen to her, but not to interfere with her idea. She needs an adult to find appropriate music, take her to school, help her prepare furniture in the room and ask Charlotte to watch the dance.

Without adult help, her dance idea would not have developed so that it was translated into a dance and shared with Charlotte. Four-year-olds often manage to draw pictures and give them to people as gifts. It is more difficult to give a dance as a gift without help. This was part of Hannah's zone of potential development

Play and its important contribution to the zone of potential development

Vygotsky believes that what a child can do with help today, she will be able to do by herself tomorrow. Play is one of the most important ways in which young children are able to develop child–initiated, self–directed activity. Play makes a deeply important contribution to the zone of potential development.

> In play a child always behaves beyond his average age, above his daily behaviour; in play it is as though he were a head taller than himself. As in the focus of a magnifying glass, play contains all developmental tendencies in a condensed form and is itself a major source of development.
>
> (Vygotsky, 1978: 102)

Adults need to develop skills in recognising when children need to be independent and when they need help.

Various children are attracted to the play props on the table, with their hints of possible stories and play scenarios to be created. Two children soon get together and a story begins to emerge. Other children gather around the table, and the teacher joins them to give backstage support to the stories the children begin to create.

Three-year-old **ANTHONY**, playing with the doll's house and talking to himself, needs to be alone. He is, with physical props, telling himself a story. At a later stage he will try to write stories and will need plenty of adult help at that point.

In this next example adult support was needed during the play.

> A group of three- and four-year-olds playing shoe shops needed an adult constantly in attendance in order to sustain the theme of the play scenario and the characters they adopted in the role play. **NEELAM** (four years) was a customer and the adult was the shopkeeper. The children began to join in, having observed what the adult and Neelam were playing. The adult invited children to try on shoes, addressing them as if they were customers. Neelam decided to be the shopkeeper and took the money, gave change and bills, and so on. The adult became a customer in order to make way for her. At one point, the adult was called away, and the play scenario collapsed.
>
> Four-year-old **NISHAM** would not let anyone have the football boots to try on, and a quarrel broke out. When the adult returned, he agreed to be the shopkeeper again and let children put the shoes on briefly. In this way, he kept control of the football boots, but let other children try them on too! This game was clearly in the children's zone of potential development and needed a coordinator – the adult.

In this section of the chapter the focus has been on developing intrinsic motivation in children. The role of practitioners is a crucial part of this process, as are the ways in which play is supported and extended.

5 Self-discipline is emphasised as the only kind of discipline worth having. Reward systems are very short term and do not work in the long term in developing the moral and spiritual aspects of living. Children need their efforts to be valued and appreciated

Vygotsky believes that when children are involved in imaginative play they will renounce what they want, and willingly subordinate themselves to rules in order to gain the pleasure of the play. He argues that in child-initiated play children exercise their greatest self-control.

> Three-year-old **JAMES** wanted to hold the teddy in the home corner and 'feed' him. But he allowed three-year-old Matthew to feed the teddy because Matthew was pretending to be the zoo keeper. In order that the play could progress he gave up what he wanted.

This principle links with Principle 4. James initiated the constraints on himself in the play. He voluntarily and willingly gave up what he wanted for the play scenario to be sustained. Play encouraged him to see things from the point of view of what was important for Matthew in keeping the play going. In a play situation he was able to show great self-discipline (Bruce, 2004). Children need clear boundaries. If they do not find them they begin to test out situations that are inconsistent or unclear, and they quickly become insecure and unanchored. Predictable environments make children feel safe. They know where they are with adults. This is closely linked with the development of dispositions for learning (Katz and Chard, 1993) mentioned earlier in the chapter.

Children are better able to explore and follow their interests in worthwhile ways in a predictable environment with clear boundaries. This is very different from controlling children through external techniques. Marion Dowling (2000) gives this example:

> In one study in a nursery school, a group of children were provided with drawing materials and told they would receive a prize for drawing which, in due course, they did. Another group were given the same materials, but with no mention of prizes. Some time after, drawing was provided as one of a range of optional activities. Significantly the children who chose to spend least time on drawing were those who had been previously rewarded.

Adults can encourage children to do what adults want through giving rewards or punishments. For example, the use of star charts for individual children is widespread. The 'marbles in a jar' reward system is also widely used. Children are rewarded for completing classroom tasks (such as tidying up quickly) with a class treat when the jar is full. These are positive reward systems. Others are negative reward systems, which punish unwanted behaviour. An example is 'Golden Time'. All children have a sun by their name on a chart. If they misbehave they are warned and a cloud is placed by their name. If they repeat the misdemeanour, the sun is removed and only the cloud remains. At the end of the session, children with suns by their names have a choice, at 'Golden Time', of activities that are seen as treats. This, more often than not, gives a message that to write or engage in mathematical problem solving or a scientific experience is not a treat, while playing with an expensive toy is.

The problem is that neither positive nor negative reward systems help children to reflect, analyse or think about why they want to do things or behave in particular ways that move them forward in their moral development. It might have a short-term favourable result, but in the long term, encouraging self-discipline to develop is more effective. In life it is important to be self-disciplined and to think for yourself about how to behave, rather than to have your behaviour controlled by and rewarded by others as a crowd to be herded.

6 There are times when children are especially able to learn particular things

Anyone who spends time with children will know that at different stages they seem to be much more interested in some activities than others.

> Seven-year-old **WILLIAM** was intensely keen on skateboarding for several months, as well as being fascinated by bows and arrows, aeroplane flight paths, sledging, roller skating, BMX bike riding, tiddlywinks and ice skating.

> Three-year-old **KATE** made a model of her classroom out of bricks and junk material. She put the 'furniture' in a cardboard box on its side. She kept infilling more furniture and people until there was no more floor space left. During the same week she went to the newspaper box and spread sheets of it all over the floor. She said she was making a road. She had a pancake for tea and spread sugar, jam and lemon juice all over it with meticulous care and then did not want to eat it, even though she loved pancakes!

These are manifestations of what Piaget has called schemes or 'schemas' (in William's case a trajectory schema and in Kate's an infilling one). Piaget says (Piaget and Inhelder, 1969: 4) that a schema is 'the structure of organisation of actions as they are transferred or generalised by repetition in similar or analogous circumstances'. The importance of the schema to the early childhood educator is that it provides a mechanism for analysing 'where the learner is' and helps predict other situations that will be of interest to the child.

Schemas change in complexity as the child grows up. For the first 18 months to two years they are sensori–motor (based on the senses and movement); from two years or earlier the schemas also begin to be represented symbolically, in alignment with the development of cause–and–effect relationship (known as functional dependency).

> One-year-old **AMANDA** paints a line. This is a sensori-motor action. At 18 months, she is calling a line she draws 'Doggy' immediately after seeing a dog. This is using the line or trajectory schema at a symbolic level of functioning.
>
> Four-year-old **DAVID**, having just painted a thick line on the paper, changes paint brushes. He now draws a thin line. 'See this brush?', he asks. 'It's fat. This one's thin. Look!' He uses each in turn and laughs. 'Fat,' he says, pointing to the line the thick brush made. He has established the cause-and-effect relationship between thickness of brush and thickness of line.

Observing the network of schemas in a particular situation at a particular time, and the level at which the child is predominantly functioning, helps the early childhood educator to respond effectively during the early years of education. This aspect of Piagetian theory has been developed through the work of Chris Athey at the Froebel Institute, London, while directing the Leverhulme and Gulbenkian Research Project 1972–1976, and has been widely disseminated through in-service work and publications.

Athey (1990: 107), in her pioneer work, describes the importance and usefulness of schemas for identifying the consistent thread of interest that a child may have. This can be hidden from the educator if he or she concentrates simply on the content of the child's interest.

> … naming (if viewed from a content point of view) could be taken as instances of 'flitting'. Randolph (three and a half years), for instance, cut out a zig zag pattern to which he attached three different names: 'a bird's wing', 'a fish tail' and 'a fan'. He was 'fitting' different but appropriate content into his latest 'form'.

He could be accused of flitting but, as Chris Athey emphasises, he is fitting the content of his experiences of nature into his latest form, or schema, which is the zig zag.

One of the most frequent schemas for children aged two to five years is interest in what Piaget calls 'enclosure'. Athey gives an example of the children in the project using large wooden blocks (bricks) to build an enclosure, and then using it representationally over a short period of time as a car, boat, taxi and ambulance. In other words, the content may be flitting, but the dominant schema is not. Athey quotes (1990: 8) the example of Louise and her envelopment schema:

> Over several months, Louise systematically explored enveloping space and certain associated schemas. She always carefully wrapped things up. For instance, she wrapped her clay pancake up (it was too hot to hold). She went round covering things up. When she had covered up the windows of her model house she said: 'now it's dark inside'. She covered a worm with sand saying: 'you know they live under the sand … at night he'll be asleep'. She made a small hole right through her home book. Her mother was embarrassed and carefully mended the book. Louise made: 'a sofa with a hole in it'. She wrapped 'sausages' in tin foil to 'cook' them. She wrapped up her mother's shoes at home and 'posted the parcel' in the rubbish bin, 'the postbox'. When she arrived at school she painted 'a parcel with Mummy's shoes in it'. Using different materials, Louise told a long story (on audio tape) about her cat. The persistent theme was the cat going inside and outside the dustbin and bringing what was inside the dustbin into the house and so on. Her persistent concerns had become sufficiently internalized for her to have an interesting conversation about them.

Some of the most frequently used schemas observed by practitioners are enclosure, rotation, trajectory and grid (see Chapter 5).

7 What children can do (rather than what they cannot do) is the starting point for a child's learning

Vygotsky extends the meaning of this principle when he stresses the need to aim for the ripening structures of potential development, which require the help of adults and other children. He sees a good education as one that stresses what children can do as their capability begins to emerge. Concentrating on what children can do does not only mean emphasising what they can do unaided. It also means emphasising what they can do with sensitive, appropriate help. Just concentrating on what children can do without help undervalues the emerging competencies.

Vygotsky points out also that, given the right help, children are capable of higher levels of functioning than if they are left without assistance. Children should not be underestimated. In play with other children, the problem of underestimation diminishes, since they can set the level of complexity, control their own rules and make their own actions subservient to the meanings in the game. They can self-pace their developing abstract thinking. Vygotsky says that learning 'awakens a variety of internal development processes that are only able to operate when the child is interacting with people in his environment, and in co-operation with his peers' (1978: 90).

In play, children can operate at a higher level. The same applies when children are introduced to new activities, such as cutting with scissors, using glue and so on, with the help of an adult who extends their learning and enables them to do something that they would not be able to do on their own. During play, or in a problem-solving situation that is supported by an adult, the child is using what he or she can do. Vygotsky (1978) believes that instruction helps to bring consciousness and deliberate mastery to the child's abilities, but only provided the child is 'within the limit set by the state of his development'. Katz and Chard (1993: 30) emphasise that

> Of particular concern is the risk that introducing formal academic and direct instruction in the early years may jeopardise the development of desirable dispositions …
>
> Early achievements may threaten development of the dispositions to be readers and appliers of mathematical skills given the amount of drill and practice usually required for success in applying these skills at an early age. This issue can be referred to as the damaged disposition hypothesis.

Instruction helps to bring consciousness and deliberate mastery to the child's abilities but only provided that he or she is 'within the limit set by the state of his development'.

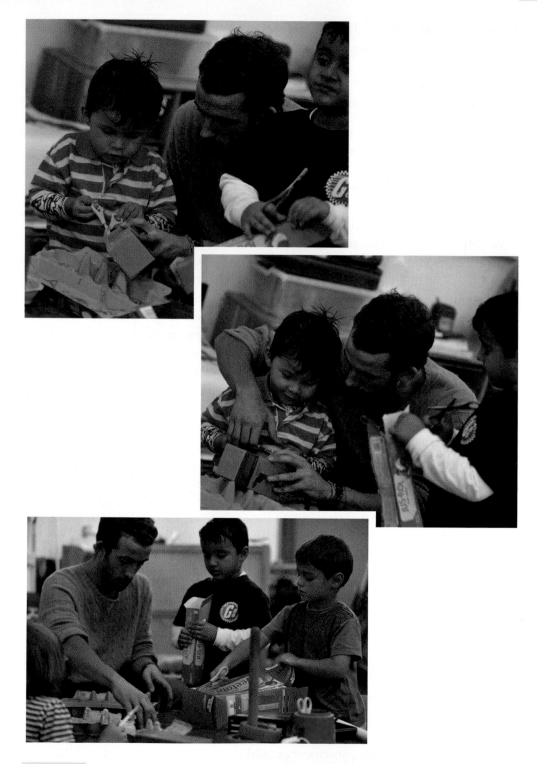

Figure 3.5: The boys are making masks, spears and shields to hunt dinosaurs.

8 Diverse kinds of symbolic behaviour develop and emerge when learning environments conducive to this are created at home, in early childhood settings, indoors and outdoors

There are two aspects to Piaget's theory:

1. stage-dependent;
2. stage-independent.

The inner life is about the way children become symbol users and represent experiences. This is of particular interest to early childhood educators. Both stage-dependent and stage-independent aspects demonstrate Piaget's fascination with the 'inner life'.

First, and largely separate from the 'inner life', there is physical experience, which involves direct, first-hand experiences (for example, playing with water through a sieve). Children find out about the properties of objects in this way, but always relating them to what they already know through a process called 'simple abstraction'. These experiences can be directly taught.

Second, there is the sort of experience that leads to what Piaget calls 'reflective abstraction'. This involves reflecting on the actions performed during direct physical experiences. This kind of experience can be facilitated but not directly taught. It involves an internal coordination and transformation of the actions that are not included in the presence of the first-hand experience. This supports the need for adults to respect the process that Bruner et al. (1976) called 'incipient intentions' or that Vygotsky refers to as the 'ripening buds'.

These processes can be facilitated by the provision of appropriate concrete activities: adults can 'scaffold' the activity, as Bruner suggests, or teach at the point of emergence of structures, as Vygotsky requests. But it is within the child that thinking is coordinated and transformed. Adults cannot think for children and transfer these thoughts to them by direct transmission. They can only help children to think for themselves. Thus, to some extent, helping children to learn is necessarily an act of intuition. It is an act of intuition because there is not much tangible feedback from these internal processes, especially with children of birth to six years of age. This is also often true of children with disabilities and complex needs. The practitioner has to rely on clues from the child that the experience is feeding the inner processes (Nielsen, 1992). The inner life is crucial to early childhood practice, including as it does the construction of images, the reconstruction of experiences, symbol use, and imagination and play – the ability to go beyond the here and now.

The adult observes the child, and tries to tune in to the child's thinking (what Bruner calls the 'incipient intention of the child').

9 Relationships with other people (both adults and children) are of central importance in a child's life, influencing emotional and social well-being

Kellmer Pringle stresses relationships, emphasising feelings (love, security, appreciation and recognition). Vygotsky, Bruner and Piaget also stress relationships but emphasise cognition (thinking).

* In Vygotsky's view, it is from social interaction that higher functioning develops.
* Bruner has increasingly come to value the adult/child partnership, particularly in relation to problem-solving and developing attitudes that facilitate the process.
* Piaget emphasises the part played by culture in the process of social transmission. In this way, the child does not have to reinvent that which is already known. This links with recent work on the importance of social as well as biological evolution.

(Bruce, Meggitt and Grenier, 2010)

Early childhood traditional practice has often been perceived as emphasising the affective (feelings) aspects of development, and Kellmer Pringle is in that tradition. More recently, support for this foregrounding of the importance of emotional and social development has come from the neurosciences (Damasio, 2004), but it is also crucial to recognise the central role of thinking and to include theories that resonate with the current work on relationships and well-being (Gopnik et al., 1999), thereby balancing the lenses through which we look at child development.

Although Vygotsky puts the main emphasis on cognition, affect is important in his theory. The satisfaction and enjoyment of playing with others, the closeness of an adult/child partnership, are not, in fact, purely cognitive. The sensitivity of Bruner's adult/child partnership echoes this implicit affectivity. Piaget (1968) is quite open in asserting that the life of the mind cannot be dichotomised into affect and cognition. Everything interweaves. People and relationships are, albeit implicitly, central in his theory.

Relationships are key to development in each of the four approaches, and this paves the way for the support and extension of the tenth Principle, which states the importance of the interaction of the child's internal structures both within the child's brain and body as complex networks develop, and with the environment represented by both people and things.

> 10 Quality education is about three things: the child, the context in which learning takes place, and the knowledge and understanding that the child develops and learns

We have seen that Bruner suggests good practitioners tune in to the 'incipient intention' of the child and act accordingly.

Bruner's thinking has developed over the years. He now gives greater stress to the context in which learning takes place and puts more emphasis on the partnership between the child and the adult, but the adult's sensitivity to the child's thinking and ideas remains central.

> So much of learning depends upon the need to achieve joint attention, to conduct enterprises jointly, to honour the social relationship that exists between learner and teacher, to generate possible worlds in which propositions may be true or appropriate, or even felicitous; to overlook this functional setting of learning whatever its content is to dry it to a mummy.
>
> (Bruner, 1977: xiv)

This means knowing what the child can manage to do without help, and knowing what the child can understand but cannot yet achieve without help. We need to remember that understanding something comes before the ability to perform, at first falteringly and then with competence. Because a child cannot 'perform' or can perform only falteringly, this does not mean he or she is not ready for the task. A tottering baby is allowed to walk, and may hold someone's hand or hang on to furniture. A three-year-old may spill cookery ingredients that can be scooped up from the table. Children need to be introduced to areas of knowledge from the start, but through an appropriate environment (people, objects, places and events).

Conclusion

Whereas in the decades from the 1960s the influence on early childhood practice of the theorists introduced in this chapter was strong, from the 1980s the emphasis shifted from child development to the socio-cultural contexts of childhood learning (Dahlberg *et al.*, 1999). Recently, there has been a move towards a more balanced approach, with the importance of both the biological and socio-cultural strands of early childhood practice being acknowledged. In this book, both are given attention in ways that coordinate the two into an integrated whole. The emphasis in this chapter has been on looking at children through the lenses of some classic theories and exploring how they resonate with ten principles of traditional practice.

examples of broad material provision, both outdoor and indoor. It is important not to let emphasis on material provision lead to under-emphasis on the child.

The important thing for early childhood educators to remember is, how will the provision be used to serve the child, and how will it help the adult to help children develop further their ideas, feelings or relationships, movement and embodiment. It depends where and when children grow up, and whether or not they attend group settings before the age of six or seven years. Many children are at home during these years in many parts of the world. Where children do join early years groups, it is important to bear in mind that material provision, together with the people they spend time with, are the essence of the early years environment indoors and outdoors.

The environment in which children develop and learn involves the people with whom the child interacts, the objects or material provision they encounter, and the places and events experienced. The way that children are helped to develop skills in using what is provided, and the way they are helped to develop competence and mastery and dispositions and attitudes that aid learning, are of crucial importance. The environment is the mechanism by which the early childhood educator brings the child and different aspects of knowledge together. 'Observing, supporting and then extending' (Bruce, 1987: 65) is the key to good learning.

The following should be offered every day. Most can be provided both inside and outside:

* workshop area for making and creating;
* woodwork;
* painting;
* drawing, mark-making, writing and book making;
* wooden blocks;
* home corner and dolls;
* sewing;
* food preparation;
* book corner (warm, light and cosy);
* small world and doll's house;
* computer;
* movement dance, drama and music space;
* climbing frames;
* bikes and wheeled vehicles;
* sand, water, malleable material (clay and dough);
* dressing-up clothes;
* gardening and nature study;
* puzzles;
* interactive display/interest table/wall display;
* digging area.

Figure 4.2: Examples of daily material provision structured to encourage an interactionist way of learning.

Figure 4.2:   *Continued*

Interest tables and displays

These are an aspect of material provision that requires care. The central aim is to:

* give children direct experiences;
* allow their initiatives and extend them;
* support intrinsic motivation broadly and in depth;
* facilitate the development of dispositions and attitudes that are helpful to learning.

Therefore children must be allowed to interact with the interest table and help to make interactive displays. These things cannot be static.

Some early years educators make available a wall near the drawing/writing area where children can put up their work if they wish. Sometimes an activity becomes an interest table after it has finished (for example, cooking apple pie). A recipe book, utensils and ingredients are put on an interest table near the home corner, and children are likely to try to cook or to touch. In this way the children can reflect on, and use, what they have learned, and practise and consolidate their learning free from adult domination. In this way, interest tables and activities blend towards future worthwhile knowledge.

Documentation is discussed in Chapter 6 (see the section on Reggio Emilia) and this can easily be incorporated into the way that displays are developed.

Themes, topics and projects

These are another way of approaching material provision. However, most early childhood educators who use a topic, theme or project approach do not take up the children's initiatives. They simply decide on a topic, which seems to be plucked out of the air rather than based on and informed by observation of individual children. This is more in keeping with the empiricist transmission model of development and learning. It does not support the principles of the early childhood traditions.

When adults use observation as the base of their record-keeping system (Bartholomew and Bruce, 1993; Drummond, 1993; Carr, 2001; Edgington, 2004; Hutchin, 2010), a topic or theme can be an added source of interest and learning for children, and can serve as a useful backdrop. However, it is by no means necessary and many early childhood educators prefer to use their child observations to inform their planning without introducing a theme that seems to them contrived, and adds another layer of work for practitioners, often without great benefit to the children's development and learning.

The development of mastery and skills

Skills and competencies (mastery) are considered at some length here because this is not looked at as an entity elsewhere in the book. The key message is that the early childhood practitioner should introduce skills that the child needs in order to become increasingly competent and be in a position to use.

Using scissors

When an adult sits each child down in turn and 'teaches' him or her to cut and then ticks the skill off on a check-list, the activity lacks function, purpose or meaning for the child. It does not build on what the child initiates or is implicitly trying to do. It makes an error into something to be avoided, and there is a complete absence of any negotiation of shared contexts and meanings with the adult. In fact, this approach is totally at odds with the early childhood tradition.

Figure 4.3: Using an interactionist approach, the boy learns to use scissors to cut the tomato plants in the garden.

Writing names

Skills need to be taught and mastery encouraged, but this needs to be in an embedded context that relates to what children strive to do. The same principles apply when children are learning to tie their shoelaces, cut their food at mealtimes, swim, draw or write their name. Having a sense of control and mastery is deeply linked with self-confidence and feelings of self-esteem (Roberts, 2002).

For instance, the moment to introduce correct letter formation, established through groundbreaking work by Ferreiro (Ferreiro and Teberosky, 1983; Ferreiro, 1997) is when children try to write their names, or their first 'fixed string'. In Chapter 7, it is suggested that the first fixed string is the moment when children resolve the conflict between their own personal symbols and those that can be shared with others. At this point, the child can see the purpose of legibility, speed, formation and aesthetic quality.

Athey (1990) found that when children begin to use clear semi-circles in drawing and to use emergent writing it is an indication of readiness to tackle lower-case letter formations, provided the understanding that written forms are made out of fixed strings is also emerging, as Ferreiro suggests. At this point, direct teaching gives children the skills needed to undertake legible, speedy and well-formed handwriting, which will usefully serve the writing process.

Tracing, using templates or stencils, completely cuts across this process and is contrary to the principles of early childhood education. It is more in keeping with the transmission model of education. Being able to represent someone else's idea of a cat by means of a stencil is low-level work. It keeps children busy, but it has little to do with education. Helping children to use what they can do – draw circles and lines – tells them that they can draw their own cat, which is unique and imaginative. This is a higher-level skill in the child and needs careful encouragement from adults.

A class of six-year-olds had fully established the repertoire of marks on paper that are needed to form letters in the English language. (Some languages use lines predominantly, some curves, for the written form. Written English uses mainly lines for capitals and a mixture of lines and curves for lower case.) This class was involved in a project on the Middle Ages, stemming from an interest in castles by a group of children in the class. Each child wrote his or her name and decorated the first letter. Some moved on from this to write poems, which they later presented beautifully. The aesthetic possibilities of handwriting were highlighted in this way. Mastery and skill in presenting work and sharing it with others became appreciated.

Three-year-old **PAUL** sat in the book corner. He picked up a book and ruffled it, dropped it and opened it in the middle. The practitioner sat with him and opened it, explaining about beginning where the story starts. She helped him to look at it so that he could benefit from the experience. At story time she used a book with an enlarged text with a group of children. She asked Paul to show her how to begin and Paul was pleased with his success. He liked becoming skilled in the use of books. Lack of skills brings lack of confidence.

Eight-year-old **HANNAH** and six-year-old **WILLIAM** went with their parents to a barn dance in the local park. Hannah joined in with gusto after initial hesitation. She had in fact learnt to 'do-si-do' at school during country dancing. The following week the family went again, and this time William joined in. He was meticulous in getting the 'do-si-do' exactly right and would only take part in partner dances with the family, so that he could get it correct.

A few days later Hannah made up a dance at home using a pop song. In it she used some of the steps she had learned when barn dancing. The newly acquired skills were being incorporated into a new dance context, choreography. There are links here with creativity (Bruce, 1991).

It is important that equipment is readily available for children to practise their newly acquired skills. If the woodwork bench is put out only once a week, it is not possible for children to regularly practise woodwork. Children need opportunities in becoming proficient when they are ready, not when educators are ready. If children use climbing frames only once a week, the 'ripening structures' Vygotsky talks about are not adequately catered for in the environment. In situations where skills and the dispositions towards learning are not encouraged, accidents are more likely (Bruce, 2004).

The ways in which materials are set out, the range and variety of materials offered, the way adults help children to learn how to use materials, are all important in encouraging children to represent.

* It is necessary to have some anchor areas always in the same places and forms, for example the book and home areas. Other areas might change regularly to link with recent experiences that the children have had as a group, for example a visit to the park.
* Different kinds of material make different demands. Children need to experience the challenge of many experiences and a wide range of materials.

This is an important reason why children need to have access to outdoor play every day. The clumsy child needs to become more proficient in using the shoulder, because the shoulder affects the movement of the arms and hands (Bruce, Meggitt and Grenier, 2010). The woodwork bench, climbing frames and dancing outside are excellent provision for this need. So are situations involving searching for ants' nests or looking at worms. Children learn to be gentle in their movements as they are taught not to harm creatures, and to return them to their habitat.

Places, events and culture

Places and events that are part of the cultural background are also important aspects of the context of learning environments. For example, visiting horse stables, the mosque, museums, the train guard's van, or the park and shops, being visited by a puppet group or studying Diwali, are all important. The context is both indoors and outdoors beyond the early years setting. We experience places, events and culture influenced by the people with whom we spend time.

People

People are an important central part of a child's development and learning. The contribution made by both adults and other children is stressed throughout this book. The child's family and socio-cultural backgrounds are deeply influential. Children do not leave the socio-cultural aspects of their lives behind when attending a group or school. Their culture and the people they live with are a part of them (Rogoff *et al.*, 2003; Bruce, 2004).

The content of the child's learning

What children learn is culturally defined. There are stark contrasts between the content of the National Curriculum in, for example, Norway, New Zealand, Reggio Emilia or in the Pacific Rim. Early childhood practitioners need to be informed about the culture in which they work and its curriculum emphasis, but thinking about the knowledge children acquire is also enhanced by knowing how other cultures approach the growth of knowledge and understanding, and how narrowly or holistically the concept of curriculum is viewed. Some cultures emphasise performance according to teacher-led tasks, while others place more emphasis on reflective, critical, imaginative and creative aspects (Miller and Pound, 2010).

Early childhood practice in action

This chapter so far has given a broad framework for approaching the 'three Cs' of the child's learning environments created both indoors and outdoors:

* the child;
* the context;
* the content.

In addition, certain basic elements in the learning process need to be built in, namely breadth and depth of knowledge and the pursuit of excellence, with high expectation for each child. What is offered in the learning environment indoors and outdoors needs to be relevant and to have meaning for the child as it is experienced.

The remainder of this chapter gives a series of examples of the early childhood curriculum in action, which brings out the points made so far. Early childhood settings, where both adults and children are active learners together, are likely to create learning environments of quality. This is not the case when adults dominate learning, or children are left to learn without adult support. Worksheets seriously constrain the learning of children because adults control what the children do from a distance, but children cannot develop their own thinking.

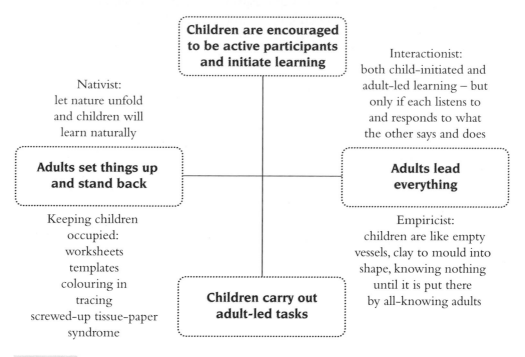

Figure 4.4: The different ways in which adults work with children.

Figure 4.5: The adult is talking with the child, who is exploring the wooden blocks and crawling off them. The interest the adult is showing sustains the concentration of the child.

A quality learning environment:

* sees adults and children as active learners;
* has staff with higher qualifications, staff with leadership skills and long-serving staff (EPPE, 2003);
* has trained nursery teachers working alongside and supporting less-qualified staff (EPPE, 2003);
* engages children both broadly and deeply with the content of the curriculum;
* has high expectations of what children do and high expectations of the learning opportunities adults provide for children;
* is based on narrative observation of children;
* emphasises adults knowing and understanding how children develop and learn (EPPE, 2003);
* has adults who are informed about the area of learning to be studied (the content);
* emphasises the need for adults to be informed also about the context in which learning takes place so that children are given access in which their learning is both supported and extended – this is particularly important in relation to equality of opportunity;
* uses observation (assessment and evaluation) to inform the planning of the curriculum so that adults begin with observation and move to support and consolidate what they learn, and also extend the learning into less familiar aspects of knowledge and understanding;
* recognises that a depth of knowledge is important to the teacher if he/she is to respond flexibly to the child's interest – every area of the curriculum has a particular pattern, order, set of relationships within it.

Conclusion

The learning environment builds on three elements: these include the biological processes of child development and learning, the socio-cultural context in which development and learning take place, and the areas of knowledge to which the child is introduced. In a quality learning environment indoors and outdoors these come together in an integrated way.

The key to developing learning in early childhood is that adults should (Bruce, 1987: 65):

* observe the child;
* support the child in developing and learning;
* extend the child's development and learning.

5 Schemas

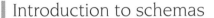

Introduction to schemas

Schemas are biologically determined patterns in the way babies and young
children behave. Knowing about them helps practitioners, parents and carers
to understand children better and to be more sensitive to their ideas, thoughts,
feelings, relationships, self-embodiment and physical needs. Perhaps most
importantly, however, understanding schemas also helps adults to relate to
children more easily and to enjoy their company more, as well as helping the
children to learn in deep and thorough ways.

A schema is:

> a pattern or repeatable behaviour into which experiences are assimilated
> and that are gradually co-ordinated. Co-ordinations lead to higher-level
> and more powerful schemas.

> (Athey, 1990: 37)

Children do not act randomly but in ways that are patterned, through the
influence of their genetically pre-determined biological development and also
through the way socio-cultural influences interact with their biological make-up.
Beneath the apparent randomness and chaos in a child's behaviour there is order
(Gleick, 1988).

The more we learn about the developing brain, the more the interactions
between biological patterns and socio-cultural influences need to be emphasised.
Nurture shapes nature (Blakemore, 2000). This means that the people we meet
and the experiences we have impact on our biological development. The way
schemas are supported or constrained influences which aspects become strongly
developed and which do not.

The pioneering work of Chris Athey

The study of schemas began in the UK in the 1970s. The work was first
pioneered by Chris Athey, who was Leverhulme/Gulbenkian Research Fellow
for the Froebel Nursery Research Project, 1972–77, based at the Froebel
Institute. The author was the teacher at the school set up in the grounds of the
Froebel Institute College to focus on working with parents in a close partnership,
and together learn about children's schemas within the context of traditional
good nursery practice.

It is very important to stress that schemas should not be studied in isolation from other aspects of the child's development and learning, but within the context of traditional good nursery practice and a high-quality curriculum. The findings of the Froebel Nursery Research Project were published in book form in 1990 in a seminal work by Chris Athey, *Extending Thought in Young Children: A Parent–Teacher Partnership*.

Schemas give practitioners and parents words for what is intuitively known

Often when people begin to study schemas they exclaim: 'But I know all of this. I just never used this terminology to describe it.' One of the problems early years educators have had during the past 100 years is difficulty in expressing and articulating in words what good practice is, and what two to five year olds in particular can do. Those who can speak and write effectively and clearly about their work, as well as put it into practice, are more likely to be listened to. The study of schemas helps early childhood practitioners to develop a vocabulary of observation that in turn informs curriculum planning.

Schemas are not isolated: they develop in clusters and are part of whole networks in the brain

Schema clusters in the brain seem at times to dominate what the child does, and at other times it is as if they have gone into hibernation. At first it was thought that one schema was dominant for a period of time in a child's development. As the Froebel Nursery Project developed, and in subsequent years as more practitioners have begun to study schemas in their own early years settings and the New Zealand Council for Educational Research (Meade with Cubey, 1995) has undertaken research into schemas, it has become clear that schema clusters dominate for a time, with contextual influences and sociocultural aspects raising others from periods of quiet. This fits with recent brain studies which suggest that the brain is stimulated by use (Athey, 1990; Greenfield, 2000).

Schemas are an observation tool – but not the only one

Schemas help us to add to our knowledge of child observation (Louis, 2008). The importance of practitioners being informed by developing the lenses through which they assess and work with a child's development and learning is stressed throughout the book. Understanding schemas and learning how to observe them has emerged out of a time-honoured tradition that uses narrative observation:

* to describe what children are doing and saying;
* in interpreting and analysing what is happening using currently available theory;
* in planning the next steps in a child's learning.

Susan Isaacs used observation in this way in her famous Malting House School in the 1930s, analysing her observations using as the lens through which she interpreted them, the then-current psychoanalytic theory of Melanie Klein.

Practitioners need to use their observations to plan next steps in learning for individual children according to their individual needs as well as those of the group as a whole. The tradition of observation and analysis continues from Susan Isaacs until today.

The basis of good teaching is informed observation. Once observed and identified, knowing about the schema clusters that children have can help practitioners and parents or carers to plan interesting and appropriate learning experiences.

Schemas should not be viewed in isolation from other aspects of observation or good practice. Schemas enhance existing and well-tried observation strategies and will be useful to practitioners only if used in an integrated way, alongside what is already known about observation, good early years practice and a high-quality curriculum. They provide another lens to enhance our ability to tune in to children in an individual way. They should never replace other observation lenses.

Schemas are part of being human: the biological and socio-cultural paths of development

There are two paths of a child's development: the biological path and the socio-cultural path.

* **Biological aspects** – schemas have both aspects. A baby is born with a repertoire of schemas that are biologically pre-determined and that, as they mature, coordinate, integrate, transform and ripple out into ever more complex and sophisticated forms.
* **Socio-cultural aspects.** The socio-cultural aspects of schemas are to do with the way in which experience, as opposed to biological maturation, influences the development of schemas through childhood and also through our adult lives. Because the two are in a perpetual state of interaction, each influences the other, causing changes, modifications and transformations in the way we think, feel, move and relate to others.

Schemas are part of human development

Schemas are part of human development, from birth to death, but they are not in a constant state. They are always adjusting and changing in the light of experience. This is why they are such a powerful learning mechanism.

Schemas are not a curriculum method nor a curriculum model

Children with disabilities have schemas, but are often challenged in their use and development. For example, the typical rocking of a child with autism is an example of a narrow range in the use of trajectory schemas.

> HELEN, seven years old and growing up in a musical family in England, experiences and is taught by her parents several different ways in which a violin bow can produce sounds. The development of some aspects of the trajectory schema will be particularly enriched and strengthened through her developing violin playing. The pleasure and deep satisfaction of music-making with people she deeply loves, and is loved by, is part of Helen's schematic experience.
>
> In the same way DEPEE, two years old, growing up in Sarawak, North Borneo, would experience everyone taking off their shoes on entering people's homes. From the time he can walk, inside/outside schema (with feet in and out of shoes) would be influenced by intermingling this action with the feelings of being welcomed and warmly greeted by friends and relatives, and the relaxed conversation following. Feelings of love, pleasure and this relaxed state are linked with putting feet in and out of shoes in this setting.

In many cultures adults lose this sense of ease in their bodies, but the increasing involvement with aromatherapy, massage and movement sessions, yoga, t'ai chi, Pilates and gymnastic exercise indicate that many in the UK are trying to address aspects of their schemas intuitively, which relate to embodiment and the sense of self and well-being.

Biological form and socio-cultural content

As Chris Athey (1990) emphasises, form and content both play an important part in the development of schemas. The biological (form) and the socio-cultural (content) paths are interwoven in development, continually changing each other. This is why every human is unique.

Schemas function at different levels in early childhood

* **Sensori-motor level** – through the senses, actions and movements. The sensori-motor level emerges first, but is used throughout life.
* **Symboliclevel** – making something stand for something else.
* **Cause-and-effect** – sometimes called functional dependency (if I do this, then that will happen).

The symbolic and cause-and-effect levels of schemas develop alongside each other in an integrated way, once the sensori-motor level is established, and these three levels of schematic behaviour continue to be present and to surface, influenced by the context and situations that arise throughout life.

> ✳ **The abstract or operational thought level** – manifests itself when there is increasing understanding of reversibility and transformations, and a coordinated understanding of these. This emerges over time.

Neither children nor adults stay at one level all the time

Children, like adults, do not function at one level all the time. It depends what they are doing, who they are with or where they are, how tired they are, if they are hungry or need the lavatory.

Children and adults move in and out of the different schematic levels but cannot go beyond their biological capabilities at any time. As always, the biological and socio-cultural aspects of development interact, coordinate and are integrated with each other.

The dynamic aspects of schemas involve movement and actions

The dynamic aspect of a schema is like a video film, linking thoughts together as they flow. When six-year-old Koor spins around and says 'I'm mixing a cake', this is the dynamic side of the schema.

The configurative aspects of schemas are based on perceptions and the senses

The configurative aspect is like a still photograph. When Daniella (four years of age) draws with circular scribble and points out a tangled ball of string on the floor and says 'it's the string', this is the configurative aspect of the schema. Chris Athey (1990: 37) suggests that, of the early schemas, when babies are gazing at people or objects, or following them with their eyes (tracking), 'gazing leads to knowledge of configuration. Tracking leads to knowledge of the movement aspects of objects, including self and other persons'. She suggests that babies quickly begin to coordinate these two behaviours – gazing (configurative aspects) and tracking (dynamic aspects) – integrating the two into an early network, and realise that the same person or object can be still or can move about. From the beginning, the dynamic and configurative aspects of schemas seem to coordinate and integrate with each other.

Adults tend to encourage configurative aspects of schemas

Early childhood settings, schools and parents tend to encourage the configurative aspects of schemas more than the dynamic aspects. Drawings, paintings and models are usually more celebrated than children creating dances or songs.

It is more difficult to 'keep' a dance or a song than a model. After all, the configurative often leads to a product, such as a painting of the string. This can be kept as an example of the child's work in the child's folder, or put on the wall or the display, or taken home. It might be carefully labelled with what the child said: 'it's the string'.

Whereas the configurative aspect of the schema can be 'kept', the dynamic aspect of the schema cannot. It is here and gone. Nevertheless, it contains deep thinking and has much greater possibility for transformations.

Transformations are changes into new forms, adjustments and adaptations that children need to make because they are crucial for the development of abstract thinking and memory.

Chris Athey (1990) and John Matthews (2003), using the theoretical insights that schemas give, demonstrate how children's early mark-making develops in their writing, drawings and paintings. Recently he has also looked at the way that chimpanzees show similar schemas in their development (Matthews, 2011). These echo, using different theory, the earlier findings of Rhoda Kellogg in the 1950s or Michaela Strauss in the 1970s.

MORAG (five years old) lives in Scotland. She arrives in school (Primary 1) proudly wearing a kilt in a Gordon tartan. 'This is my new kilt,' she says. In her school she is helped to value her Scottish heritage. She knows it is a Gordon tartan. It is interesting that this aspect of heritage fascinates her at this time. She has a strong concern with grids. She spends time at the water tray, sieving and using the water and fish nets. She also likes the home area windows, and peeps through the net curtains frequently. 'I can see you, it's net, so I can see you.' She is enthusiastic about sewing, enjoys simple tapestry work and willingly learns how to use the thread when directly taught by her teacher.

Grid is not her only schema, but it seems to be in particularly active use for a few weeks. There is already good classroom provision in Morag's case. The teacher enhances her interest in the tartan aspect of grid by introducing a display of tartans and helping interested children to see how tartans are constructed.

Morag began to paint tartans and people wearing them. She often mixed the colours of paints that she needed in order to make a Gordon tartan. During this time she showed little evidence of schemas such as core and radial. However, she learned to make charts showing data about the weather. In these, although grid was the framework for the chart and it gave her enormous pleasure to draw the frame, she used other schemas in the symbols that she chose to represent the sun (core and radial), rain (dab) and clouds (continuous coordinated semi-circle).

'Not flitting but fitting' (Athey, 1990)

Chris Athey (1990: 107) gives the example of Randolph who cut out a zig zag pattern. He first said it was 'a bird's wing', then 'a fish tail' and then 'a fan'. As she points out, he was 'fitting' different but appropriate content into his latest 'form' (schema).

Unless adults observe children carefully, in an informed way, they may mistakenly think a child lacks purpose, or is 'off task' when, in fact, the child is systematically learning. It is important to recognise the difference when working with young children.

Figure 5.1: Inside and outside: doing an inset jigsaw puzzle.

Figure 5.1: *Continued*. The girl is fascinated by inside and outside. She puts glue inside the box.

The historic background to how schemas came to be studied

When Froebel, Montessori and Steiner were developing their curricula, nothing was known about schemas. Because they were good observers of children, each tuned in to what children naturally do, they intuitively facilitated the children's schema clusters in the curricula they developed. A high-quality learning environment is based on the observation of what naturally interests children. It is likely to be effective, since children do not have to be goaded into participation most of the time.

Froebel

Froebel, in developing the Gifts, Occupations and Movement, Mother Songs and Garden in his curriculum, together with his study and increased knowledge of play, intuitively supported and extended the schemas in the curriculum that he developed. He was working before schemas were a known concept. His first Gift was the soft ball (Liebschner, 1991; Bruce *et al.*, 1995; Bruce, Meggitt and Grenier, 2010). The subsequent Gifts were early sets of wooden blocks, ancestors of the modern unit and hollow blocks that are now regarded as essential in a high-quality early childhood curriculum.

Children love to build towers and knock them down. The more obvious schemas used in blockplay are vertical and horizontal, lateral trajectories, enclosure, connection, on top, inside/outside, transporting, up/down, dynamic trajectories, dab, clashing trajectories. Both the dynamic (transformations) and the configurative (static) aspects of schemas were encouraged in Froebel's curriculum. Children are naturally drawn to aspects of the environment that allow for opportunities for the consolidation of schemas. As Chris Athey says (1990: 46), 'functioning improves with use'. It is almost as if children actively seek people and things in the environment that echo their schemas and encourage them in their use. Chris Athey calls this 'recognition' (1990: 69).

Froebel's curriculum encouraged children in the possibilities for both consolidation and extension of schemas. For example, a set of blocks has endless opportunities for rearrangement, new ways of setting out instructions and using schemas in ever new combinations.

Montessori

Montessori's notion of sensitive periods, drawn from the Dutch biologist, de Vries, also unwittingly facilitated the development of schemas in a child's development and learning. Unbeknown to her, for she, like Froebel, was working before schemas were known, her Exercises of Practical Life, the pink tower and the didactic materials gave highly specific and pre-structured opportunities for children to practise and repeat as they exercised their schemas. Dynamic transformations were not aspects of schemas that were encouraged in her curriculum, but configurative aspects of schemas were (Bruce, 1976).

Schemas included were trajectories, vertical, horizontal, connection, on top, inside/outside, envelopment, transporting.

Steiner

Steiner's facilitation of schemas is more akin to that of Froebel. Whereas Montessori's curriculum implicitly supports schemas, Froebel's and Steiner's curricula both support and also extend the child's schemas. Steiner's use of natural materials, drapes with which children can cover themselves, toys with the ability to be imaginatively transformed, wooden blocks or irregular shapes, beeswax to mould, block crayons and seasonal craft materials, the use of story, circle time, songs and movement games do not pre-structure or stipulate the way in which a schema is practised or exercised in the environment, but instead invite experimentation, variation and transformations of many kinds. Steiner's curriculum, like Froebel's, encourages transformation as much as configurative aspects of schemas.

Examples of facilitation of support and extension of schemas in Steiner's curriculum might be envelopment, enclosure, trajectories of all kinds, push and pull, inside/outside.

Darwin

The study of schemas has emerged from Darwin's biological theories of evolution. Gradually, the disciplines of biology, psychology and the neurosciences have moved closer to each other. In recent years, biologists and mathematicians have also influenced each other more closely, for example the biologist Richard Dawkins (1993) or mathematical chaos theorist James Gleick (1988).

Figure 5.2: This is typical of the transporting schema: buggies and bags are favourite containers that children like to use to carry things or people from one place to another.

Schemas help us to see the order behind apparent chaos and disorder in a child's behaviour (Bruce, 1991: Chapter 7). It is very helpful to parents in particular, but also to professionals working with young children, to understand that children do not act in random ways but that there are underlying patterns in what they do.

Figure 5.3: The girl is transporting her doll in the buggy.

The two-year-old indicates to her childminder that she wants to play with the box, which has a lid on it. She then concentrates deeply, using her transporting schema. Her childminder helps her by holding containers at right angles to make it easier for her to succeed. Transporting is often linked with putting things into and taking them out of containers. At first, the fact that the box has a lid on it might seem irrelevant, but she may have been attracted to it because the lid envelopes (covers over) what is inside. Later on she asked for a different box, and covered herself with shredded paper. She was interested in finding the objects enveloped in the box. She also cannot resist transporting the cones and putting them in the pot.

Her cluster of consistently strong schemas seems to be: transporting, enveloping, in and out, space as a container

The neuroscientist Damasio suggests that using both the work of Darwin and Freud gives us powerful ways of looking at human development (Damasio, 2004). Piaget also admired the work of Freud, seeing his work on social emotional development in alignment with his emphasis on cognition.

Piaget

Piaget developed his work on schemas from the 1920s over a period of 50 years, adjusting his terminology as he did so. In this book, the later terminology is used, as it is in most books referring to schemas (Athey, 1990).

By four and a half months the baby can look at an object, reach out for it, grasp and suck the object. This is a new schema cluster (hand-eye coordination). Later, the ability to use and understand the purpose of a pulley, rotation or trajectory becomes linked with these early behaviours in a more coordinated and sophisticated form.

The range of Piaget's theory

One of the reasons why it would be unhelpful only to use schemas in looking at the development and learning of young children is that every theory, including Piaget's, has its range (Bruce et al., 1995: 28; Bruce, 2004). It is important to look at the fitness of purpose of any theory, and to draw on theories that complement each other and so have some philosophical cohesion. This is very different from taking an eclectic approach where bits and bobs of different theories are taken in isolated, unconnected ways. This leads to inconsistency, confusion and to practice that constantly contradicts itself. There is work to be done in linking Piaget's schemas with other theories, but the work of interactionist theorists such as Vygotsky, Bruner, Piaget and Dunn, and the psychodynamic theorists Winnicott and Erikson, have areas that blend comfortably with each other in important respects (see Chapters 3 and 8).

Of these theories, those of Dunn and Winnicott, in different ways, address socio-emotional issues most explicitly. Vygotsky emphasises language and socio-cultural aspects of thought, while Bruner emphasises representation, cognition and the role of the adult in scaffolding a child's learning. Piaget's theory remains the most over-arching and comprehensive to date. Even so, in spite of some extensions, adjustments and modifications, it still has a narrow range and looks at socio-emotional and socio-cultural issues only implicitly. A theory that is all-encompassing has yet to be developed, and it may well be that this is not possible (Bruce, 2004).

Piaget's theory: stages and networks

The most widely known aspect of Piaget's theory is his stages of development (Bruce et al., 1995). This was seized upon because it expanded the work that had been done on normative development by pioneers such as Gesell and others during the 1930s. This concentrated on milestones in a child's development (Bruce, Meggitt and Grenier, 2010).

An example of the normative development approach would be:

* a two-year-old jumps;
* a three-year-old hops;
* a four-year-old skips.

In Piaget's more sophisticated stage theory, children move from sensori-motor (at 0 to 2 years approximately) to pre-operations (2 to 7 years) and then to complete operations (7 to 11 years) and formal operations (from 11 years onwards). The ages at which children develop have been found to be highly inaccurate, with great cultural diversity. For example, children growing up in the Swiss mountains understand and see things from different viewpoints much earlier than children growing up in a flat town. Seeing things from other points of view is part of a developing 'theory of mind' (see Chapter 8), the process by which children come to understand that they may not think exactly in the same way as someone else, because everyone is a unique individual. In fact, Piaget's stage theory (this aspect of his theory is called hierarchisation) is only one small part of his whole theory. Piaget also emphasises that a child's development progresses as a more and more complex network just as much as developing through a hierarchy of stages. His view has considerable resonance with the 'nesting principle' of Damasio (2004). Piaget also gives a central place to biological maturation, experience and the socio-cultural context. These are called the 'stage-independent' aspects of Piaget's theory. Another aspect of his independent theory is his concept of equilibration, which shows that children try things out according to what they expect and know (assimilation), and then adjust, transform and change when things are other than expected (accommodation).

Schemas are best seen as being linked with both the stage-dependent (hierarchical) side of his theory and also with the stage-independent aspects. Those using Piaget's theory have tended to draw only on selected aspects, rather than to use it holistically. It is best if it is used holistically, so that both the stage-dependent and stage-independent aspects are seen as a coordinated and integrated whole.

Schemas do not disappear in later life, but they certainly change and transform as they coordinate and integrate as networks of behaviour or concepts become ever more complex and sophisticated, and according to the socio-cultural context.

Where do schemas go after childhood and later in life?

Helping a toddler who is transporting, scattering and heaping objects everywhere by providing objects that will not break or be dangerous when thrown, such as baskets and other containers, as well as space to move about unhampered, is contributing to a child's preparation for adult life. It is doing so in ways appropriate to childhood for a toddler.

Objects look different when scattered about, or when heaped together. But they are of the same quantity even though their appearance changes. The transporting schema leads towards a concept of quantity. A toddler who has rich transporting experiences is likely to benefit as an adult and develop a sound concept of quantity. There are cross-cultural variations. Some cultures stress transporting food and transferring it from large sacks to small containers rather than buying food in pre-packaged form. Children in these cultures will differ in their early experiences of quantity and transporting in relation to this.

Schemas transform into later concepts

The way children are supported in the early use of their schemas has a deep emotional impact that remains. It is perhaps significant that Seymour Papert, inventor of the Turtle Computer, writes in his book *Mind Storms* (1980) of the way his early love of cogs at about the age of five years was encouraged by his parents. He left a transparent cover on his computer so that children could enjoy seeing the movement of the cogs. Unwittingly his parents were supporting and extending his core and radial cluster of schemas. The outcome of their support during his early childhood for the things that seemed to be fascinating to him was that in adult life he developed pioneering work on computers.

Developing language and schemas

Cathy Nutbrown (2006), building on the work of Chris Athey (1990), stresses the importance of using appropriate descriptive language that links with a child's schemas during conversations. She gives the example of Stuart, looking at a hand-operated sewing machine. He tells the teacher 'it goes round and round'. The teacher replies 'Yes, it turns, it rotates', giving him the language to support his schemas.

Often children do not immediately incorporate new words into their vocabularies, but recognition gives meaning, which leads to deepening understanding and widening vocabulary. As Marian Whitehead (2004) points out, children begin to be able to use language to comment on their world.

Schemas and the whole child

Piaget (1968) stresses that movement, thinking, feelings and relationships cannot be separated. He wishes there were not two separate words for thinking and emotion. Schemas are about the whole child. They involve the physical and spiritual development of the child as well as ideas, feelings and relationships. They adjust and develop differently according to the cultural context, but schemas are a mechanism for coordinating and integrating development and learning.

Having things that can be predicted helps young children to settle into a group setting.

AMANDIP (three years old) is new, and every day the first thing he does is to go and find two planks in the wooden block area. He holds them upright and seems reassured by this start to his day. It is like his teddy bear. This anchors him and makes him feel secure. Further observations will give clues that he has a strong vertical (up/down) trajectory schema. It turns out to be significant that he holds the planks upright every day. The vertical trajectory schema coordinates and helps him to make sense of what he finds in the nursery. It helps his feelings to be anchored and find calm as he settles in to a new environment.

Figure 5.4: A boy plays with his carer.

Schemas and friendships

JOSH wanted to make a row out of the wooden blocks (horizontal trajectory). **WANDA** came and took the end block and put it on to the tower she was building. She wanted to build upwards (vertical trajectory). Josh strongly objected and snatched back his block, accidentally knocking down Wanda's tower. A quarrel broke out, with adults needing to intervene swiftly.

It would not be helpful to emphasise the importance of sharing and working together at this moment. These children are trying to do different things. Gradually it might be possible to suggest Josh makes a row of blocks that ends at the base of Wanda's tower. This might encourage the children to coordinate vertical and horizontal trajectory schemas, but not today. Instead, each child's schema needs protection from an adult in order that each has freedom to learn.

Schemas and everyday life

Every day we wake up, get up, do things, go to bed and sleep. For a toddler and young children, teenagers and even for adults, getting dressed is a whole schematic experience. Putting on a T-shirt or pants involves going through, inside/outside, over and under, enveloping, enclosing, to name only some of the schemas.

The first dressing-up clothes that children enjoy putting on and wearing in an early years setting tend to be hats, shoes and belts. These involve very basic schemas (in, out, containment and enclosure) in great evidence when observing toddlers. Soon they enjoy wearing capes or surrounding themselves with drapes. This is envelopment.

> GEORGE (three years old) was Spider-Man for several weeks. He was almost completely covered by his clothes.

Schemas are not just to do with ideas that children are developing (pretending to be Spider-Man). They are also to do with feelings, relationships and physical development. It is an emotional experience to pretend to be someone else.

Mealtimes are very emotional for children. It is a serious sadness for a child when an adult pours custard on the treacle sponge when they had wanted it beside their sponge cake. The schema is on top or enclosure. Putting curry on the rice, rather than beside it is a similarly emotional experience for adults. If a toddler, who has just begun to take note of enclosures is given a broken round-shaped biscuit, there is likely to be a strong reaction.

There is often a fashion for wearing ponytails and plaits, and an interest in African–Caribbean hairstyles when children are developing a core and radial schema cluster. Nancy would not go to her nursery until her hair was done as she wanted it. For several months her mother had to allow extra time to plait her hair each morning.

Bedtime rituals involve schemas. It matters whether teddy is under the bed covers or on top of the pillow when the 'on top' and 'underneath' cluster of schemas is strong.

Children helping with everyday chores demonstrate their schemas

The following few examples show how important this can be, provided that children are not cajoled and nagged into helping. A positive approach is more likely to encourage children to positively want to help. Children 'recognise' what is involved in helping before they can 'perform' competently.

* **Infilling** – put the blocks in the box in patterned order.
* **Trajectory and containment** – children can sweep up sand with the dustpan and brush.
* **Trajectory** – sweep the floor or the playground. Remember the child may not be aware of the beginning and ending of the handle (trajectory), and might concentrate only on the end with the brush on it. This is an important safety factor.
* **Envelopment** – wipe over the table tops to clean them.
* **Vertical trajectory** – (inside and outside) stack the saucers and the plates in the home area and put them away in the cupboards.
* **Inside/outside containment (divided space grid)** – sort and put the cutlery away in a divided cutlery box in the home area.
* **Envelopment, inside/outside, containment, transporting** – put away the dolls in their beds in the home area.
* **Snacks and washing-up. Rotation of the taps in order to fill the jug and pour water into the washing-up bowl** – this involves containment and rotation and transporting. The soap bubbles are spheres. The dish mop might be a core and radial type. Wiping up with a tea towel involves a child in envelopment of crockery and cutlery.

Schemas and the child's sense of identity and embodiment

Children use and explore schemas first of all in relation to themselves. Babies spend time putting their hand into the mouth of those they are close to. Where do I end and where do I begin? Toddlers put the whole of their body into a cardboard box and love to climb in and out over and over again.

Children playing in dens (envelopment), willow dens and under the climbing frame in the garden of the playgroup, are outside in all weathers. This results in a rich learning environment. This demonstrates the schema cluster involving space that contains, and putting things in and out of containers.

Dens are popular, as are dressing-up clothes, when children use their whole bodies to exercise the inside schema cluster, but gradually they use objects as well as self. Going inside a den is about feelings and physical behaviour as much as it is about relationships, ideas and thoughts. Cosiness, completeness, safeness, feeling anchored, these are feelings, but also intellectual ideas are integrated within the schema clusters of envelopment, inside and outside. Recent studies of the brain emphasise that the chemistry of the brain brings feelings as well as thoughts (Greenfield, 2000; Damasio, 2004). For example, anger, frustration and joy are all associated with chemical changes in the brain.

Figure 5.5: The trajectory schema. A rocket makes the trajectory as it is ejected.

Schemas and feelings

Recent work on brain studies suggests that the electrical activity of brain cells actually brings changes in the brain's physical structure. The schema clusters are modified and changed by experiences the child has. Experience, good or damaging, brings refinement or atrophying of thinking, feelings, relationships and physical developments. Children who do not play are not exercising their schema clusters. They are therefore not firing and wiring their brains optimally. This means that they learn less (Nash, 1997: 37).

In his Foreword to *The Gears of my Childhood*, Papert (1980: vi) traces the way he developed a positive affective tone towards mathematics to the early enjoyable experiences he had playing with cogs, cars and gears. Cogs are resonant of the core and radial schema, usually very strong in four-year-olds, which he was. Emotionally and intellectually rich childhoods that allow involvement and play in natural biological schemas quite literally lead to richer brains.

Relationships, feelings and interactions between adults and children (Arnold, 2010), as well as the material provisions offered, both contribute effectively to the child's learning.

Schemas are integrated, coordinated networks of behaviour through which children can gain access to knowledge and understanding, and sort out their ideas, feelings and relationships. They are part of the way the child's brain is wired.

Birth to three matters in relation to schemas

Although not explicitly designed to empower children's schema clusters, the treasure baskets developed by Elinor Goldschmied (Goldschmied and Jackson, 2004) for sitting babies, and her bags full of objects for heuristic (exploratory) play for toddlers, do in fact lend themselves to the rich development of children's schemas.

The foundation stage in relation to schemas

In an early years setting, a teacher helped the children to extend their mathematical learning. She rigged up a pulley with a bucket and hung it above the paddling pool. Four-year-old **NAYAM** and three-year-old **SHAZIA** worked with this most of the morning. Nayam was concerned with filling the bucket before it was released. He focused on fullness, sometimes with water, sometimes with toys he had collected. Shazia, on the other hand, was concerned with holding the rope right until the bucket reached the top and then releasing it. Her interest lay in the splash, which she enjoyed enormously. She and Nayam tended to argue, as their concerns were different.

Adults can support schemas with appropriate language. With the help of the teacher, Nayam and Shazia reached a compromise by which he filled the bucket, and she hoisted and released it. The role of the adult here was, as Bruner would assert, to diagnose the incipient intention of each child in order that the mathematics in the situation could be developed. The teacher used the mathematical language of 'full' and 'empty', 'half full', 'nearly full', and so on, for Nayam.

One of the important functions of language in mathematics is that it should help children to comment on the world (Whitehead, 2010). There is a need for adults to extend learning through appropriate language in genuine conversation. Genuine conversation seems to arise more often when adults have an understanding of schemas and so tune in to what the child says (Meade with Cubey, 1995: 70; EPPE, 2003).

> **SHAZIA** had also shown great interest in the paper aeroplanes introduced by the teacher, and the balloons that were blown up but not tied, so that when released they darted across the room making a squeaky noise. These were other experiences of hold and release that added to Shazia's knowledge of trajectories. She would repeat the trajectory action with her finger where it met, using words such as 'up' and making squeaky noises in imitation of the balloon. This was a mathematical experience, but it was also non-verbal communication, spoken language related to the schemas (up) and cooperation with friends.

> Three-year-old **PERRY**'s teacher introduced paper aeroplanes and noted that Perry was fascinated by the vapour trails left in the sky by the aeroplanes that passed over the school. She brought in some streamers and he ran, with streamers unravelling behind him. She was helping him to make tangible a trajectory path rather like the aeroplane's vapour trail. By tuning in to his interests, the teacher informed her planning.

Topological schemas

Shazia and Perry were both using a repertoire of topological concepts to explore trajectories (Athey, 1990: 83–85): on top, under, over, near and far. The relationship between the bucket and the top of the pulley, the throwing of the paper aeroplane, the starting point of running with the streamer, the bucket in the water in the paddling pool, the aeroplanes landing on the floor, are all an exploration of beginning and end points, and the relationship between them, or order (Athey, 1990: 85). The topological aspects involved are proximity, separation, connection and relationships between them, or order.

Schemas inform curriculum planning

Knowing that a child is exploring trajectories is not enough. The adult can extend this exploration using different areas of knowledge, and by introducing material and engaging in appropriate language or conversations. Knowing the schema informs the adult's curriculum plans, and helps the adult to plan with appropriate selection and flexibility.

Linking schemas with mathematics, dance

However, although it is certainly true that here mathematical knowledge is being introduced that matches the child's developing schemas, these schemas could also be developed in ways that are not purely mathematical. Schemas also contain the 'stuff of dance' (Davies, 2003). The child's schemas are a resource, an access mechanism, which can be used to tackle any area of knowledge. Observing and identifying schemas informs curriculum planning. The adult needs to be aware of the child's schemas, and then to consider different curriculum possibilities and next steps in learning for the child at that stage. The adult needs to bring the two together, as Perry's teacher did in introducing the streamers, or Shazia's in introducing the pulley.

Four-year-old **KUANG** was using a remote-controlled computer toy. He wanted to push it. The adult showed him that he needed to instruct it to move forwards, backwards and sideways by pressing the appropriate key (marked with a direction arrow) and another key (marked with a number) telling it how many paces to move. He quickly understood this, and made it go forward to the end of the room. Then he wanted it to go to the other end. He picked it up and turned it round, ready to go back. The adult showed him how to use the backwards arrow to reverse the direction, but he found this intervention annoying. Kuang could deal with trajectories going in one direction, but not with reversing the direction. Reversing is a more complex level of thinking.

He was taken to see trains at Waterloo Station. Since this is a terminus, where trains reach the end of the line, they had to retrace their direction out of the station. After seeing the trains, Kuang enjoyed action songs about trains reversing their paths – for example, 'Puffer Train' and stories by Rev. W. Awdry such as *Thomas the Tank Engine*, with shunting and so on.

He was also encouraged to play games such as 'What's the time, Mr Wolf!' in which children reverse in their tracks when the 'wolf' comes. It was six months before he began to retrace his steps in games. Once he did this, he used the reverse button on the computer toy. He was using a horizontal trajectory schema in developing these understandings.

Using a selection of boxes on a display with cones, acorns, conkers, leaves, etc. to put in the boxes.

A particular interest (with Edward, a fellow enveloper) in a ring box, a box with a sliding lid and a pencil box.

She was drawn to a bowl of cornflour and water, and smothered her arms and hands in the green slime with great energy and enthusiasm.

She spent increasing amounts of time in the home area where she wore layers of dressing-up clothes.

At home she used more veils for dressing up and covered her hands in chocolate when making crispy cakes.

She was interested in the number of mattresses on which the princess slept in the story of the Princess and the Pea.

Joanne's mother, during conversations with staff about envelopment and how she and Joanne were enjoying their time together, expressed her pleasure in what she had observed and said how Joanne's activities seemed to have taken on a new meaning.

Extending the schema cluster

Kim's game – this involves the adult covering a selection of objects and asking children to guess which one has been removed. It is a popular memory game, which children enjoy.

Wrapping potatoes in foil to bake at a barbecue to celebrate Diwali (small group and adult).

She enjoyed a bowl of papier-mâché (small group and an adult).

Water play – involving polythene bags filled with water of different colours. She pummelled them until they burst.

Parcels buried in the sand tray: when she approached, the sand looked smooth and she looked disappointed. As she pressed her hands in, she discovered a parcel and her face gleamed with a smile. She opened the parcel carefully to avoid tearing the paper, and then gathered all the objects revealed, scooping and pushing the sand with her other hand to make sure nothing was missed. She found a box with a lid in which to collect the treasures until they could be shared.

Sue Rice, 1996

Symbolic behaviour has layers

Symbolic behaviour has layers that become more and more coordinated as the network strengthens. This also links with brain studies (Greenfield, 2000; Damasio, 2004). Schemas continue to be important throughout life from birth to death, as adults continue to use both the senses and the movement aspects of schemas. Actively seeking out things in the environment that echo, match and resonate biologically with schemas within the person, or raising schemas to the surface through recognition that what is 'out there' matches with internalised schema clusters, are both important socio-cultural influences on schemas.

* Dandelion clocks resonate with the core and radial schema, both configurative when still and dynamic when blown.
* A fencing tournament resonates with dynamic trajectories of all kinds.
* Written English lower-case letter formations resonate with configurative grids, semi-circles, and core and radial schemas.

Tuning into children through observing their schemas

Chris Athey (1990: 63) states:

> … most adults know when they have struck a chord in a child. The child's closely focused attention usually signifies that a good match has been made between an adult stimulus and some particular or general concern in the child.

This again links with the work of EPPE (2003) on shared sustained thinking.

NATASHA, two years old, made constructions with the wooden blocks. Each time she did this she seemed concerned that her construction should look symmetrical at each end.

She was videoed in the nursery making these constructions while her family worker sat alongside her, gently protecting her block play by his presence. Other children came and appeared interested in her construction.

As soon as the video was shown to Natasha's mother, she recognised her concern for symmetry, and linked it with the mathematical concept of quotity (the kind of twoness that has symmetry). She loved to hold two identical objects, one in each hand, and to set them down opposite each other. Wooden block play lends itself to experimentation with quotity. Adults were able to be more sensitive to her.

Because the practitioner and parents shared what they knew of Natasha's interest in symmetry, they were able to be more sensitive to her both at home and the early years setting.

Natasha's mother felt justly proud of her daughter's mathematical achievements, and this warmth was felt by Natasha. The family worker felt that his work with Natasha was being valued by her family.

Piaget says that we have a network, a repertoire of behaviours (which he calls schemas – see Chapter 5) that influence what we are interested in at the time, and that alter and modify in the light of feedback from real socio-cultural experience. This means that the biological aspects of our development interact with the socio-cultural side of development, and so each of us is a unique person. This is confirmed by recent evidence from the neurosciences (see Bruce, 2004).

Piaget thought that the process of representation developed rapidly from toddler times until after the start of statutory schooling, which in most countries is appropriately six or seven years of age. This is the period when the process of representation really begins to flourish. For Piaget, as for Bruner, there is an important network of processes developing in the child, each of which interacts with the others in a web-like way.

It is a network or web that involves a child in:

* active learning;
* imitation;
* memory;
* making images, which might be auditory (sound), visual, touch, smell or taste;
* making symbols, when something stands for something else.

Imitation

Piaget does not mean copying when he says that imitation is important as part of representing experience. Imitation differs from copying in that the child makes use of and reconstructs an event after the event.

> Three-year-old **WILLIAM** sees a friend, two-year-old **CHARLOTTE**, eat cheese on toast cut into small squares in a grid pattern. He usually has toast fingers. Next day he asks for his honey toast to be made like Charlotte's. He is reconstructing in the light of a new situation and context. He is adapting an idea he wants to use.

Through imitation of this sort, children experiment with different behaviours, roles, ways of painting, swimming and much more. This is a strong argument for not separating educational provision for three- and four-year-olds since the younger children benefit from imitating the older, who in turn benefit from the leadership and sense of responsibility involved. The practice of mixing three- and four-year-olds is currently being eroded. Piaget's notion of imitation gives strong justification for the mixing of ages.

Figure 6.7: The first dressing–up clothes that children enjoy are usually hats and shoes. The adult is encouraging play with ideas about what can become a hat, with a bit of imagination.

Figure 6.8: Den building seems to happen all over the world. There is a surge of it in this group of children; sometimes dens are made indoors, and, as in this situation, they are often found outdoors.

Vygotsky says that the child, such as Sadiq, sees one thing (the daisy) but acts differently towards it (treating the daisy as if it were an egg). He gives the daisy a different meaning. That is what children do when they make something into a play prop.

The theories we have looked at in this chapter, of Bruner, Winnicott, Piaget and Vygotsky, lead us to some practical strategies. We have established that children need direct, powerful, emotional experiences, and a consistent environment that offers diverse, enriching opportunities. Young children require a supportive setting in which imaginative play is encouraged, through which there is frequent opportunity to reflect.

Some practical strategies for encouraging the development of representation

Recent research emphasises the importance of context, both in social relationships and the influences of the culture.

Throughout this book, the advantages of younger and older children playing together are emphasised. Vygotsky's and Piaget's work shows how important it is for younger children to see older children handling materials with confidence and pleasure, and to see moments of struggle and recognise how the adults in the environment are supportive and enabling at such times. Motivation to learn and move forward is closely linked with security, self-confidence and self-esteem. Adults can help children in these areas.

Figure 6.9: At first it looks as if the boys are aimless but, as the practitioner observes them, it becomes apparent that they are making a play scenario that involves checking for monsters. There is plenty of discussion as they go about the sort of places monsters might hide and why. They use the whole outdoor area, which supports the development of spatial concepts and lays the foundation for map work.

Observing children

Careful child observation comes first, as illuminated by Matthews (2003) so that the emphasis is on looking at and identifying what the child can do, before leaping into action. Adults working with children will also need to act on their observations of children (see Chapter 11).

The adult first observes the child's themes of play, drawing, models, conversations and so on, then attempts to help children individually, or as a group, to elaborate these themes. This might be through conversation, through suggestion, or by providing relevant and appropriate materials and experiences in a sensitive way. There is a world of difference between intervening sensitively and appropriately and interfering when adults move into teaching without first tuning in to the child.

Working with young children, providing appropriate materials and experiences, might also mean that adults need to allow themselves to be used as an extension of the child – for example, holding the sticky tape while children cut it, to stop them from giving up at a difficult moment, or helping to keep a theme going in the home corner when the play is breaking down.

Two three-year-olds, **BARBARA** and **CLARE**, wanted to play nurses, but a quarrel broke out over who should give out the medicine. The adult intervened, saying 'I am the sister. Nurse Barbara, would you take the patient's temperature? Nurse Clare, please would you wash the patient?' Both are given attractive nurse-like tasks. The adult has kept the theme and the roles going and has also extended the children's play in adding to the range of nurse-like activities.

Materials that can be used for representation

Material provision (which is explored in more detail in Chapter 4) involves people, events and objects with which the children interact. It can be set out in many ways to excite curiosity and surprise, and yet there must be security for the children. Different kinds of provision make different demands. Children need to experience the challenge of many different experiences, and of wide-ranging provision.

At three years old, **HANNAH** danced a rosebud unfurling. This was her idea. She was very frustrated when she tried to draw this event.

It is important to bear in mind Bruner's three modes of representation, and the conflicts the child must resolve between them. This implicitly argues for a rich, wide range of media for young children to experience and work with.

Children need to become proficient in the representational possibilities of different clays, doughs and woodwork as well as plasticine, mud and wet sand.

They need different papers, brushes and paints, from oil to poster to powder paint, thick, thin and medium. They need to draw with pastels, charcoal, pencils, felt pens, chalks, inks and so on.

Children need to experience and tell stories, hear and see and make music, and dance in different styles – dramatic, comforting, romantic, folk – from different cultures. Endless possibilities emerge. Depending on the material, the representational experience and degree of symbol use will be entirely different each time. For example, it will be very difficult for Georgio (four years old) to make a representation of his bathroom pipe freezing and bursting (a dramatic experience for him and his family) in clay, woodwork, sand, dance or drama, but he managed to do it at the water tray.

It is important for children to try out what it is like to represent in different ways with different materials. A broad material range becomes exciting and interesting for adults to provide and watch and help children to use when representing. Some children will show more strength in one area, less in another. Others will be all-rounders.

WILLIAM, at three years old, almost never paints, although the opportunity is constantly available. He rarely draws, either. He rejects dough and clay. But he models a blackbird out of plasticine, with a black body, head, wings, a yellow beak, two yellow eyes, and yellow legs and feet. He is angry when it will not stand up, and only grudgingly accepts the suggestion that it could sit on a nest made by a helpful adult. He wants it to hop. The representation of movement is what he really wants. He knows that blackbirds have a springy hop. He represents this with his body, briefly, before a rough-and-tumble game develops with his sister. William prefers to represent using three dimensions, and through dance-like movements.

KATE, at three and a half years, rarely drew or painted, but made marvellous models. She made a model of her school classroom one day with a cardboard box and bricks to represent furniture, accurately placed spatially.

Interestingly, at five years old, both these children were doing meticulous and beautiful drawings and two-dimensional work, but both were easily frustrated if their efforts did not work out. Kate went on to study art at A-level and William studied physics.

It is easier to change clay or bricks and reorganise them than it is to change a drawing that has not gone according to plan. On the other hand, it is easier to fall into a stereotyped and narrow formula in drawings, and to let dance-like musical and three-dimensional work atrophy as the imagination increasingly fails. Kate and William were encouraged in the early years (0–8 years) to experiment, explore and value their own personal idiosyncratic representations. They were not 'forced' to adopt cultural conventions or to draw in formulas. In this way they made use of conventional symbols and ways of representing while developing their own personal symbols with imagination and creativity.

Representation in all its forms is important. Dance, music, sculpture, construction toys, drawing, painting, mathematics, making scientific theories, literature and drama all offer different possibilities. Each offers something special, something worthwhile and unique. We can keep hold of past experiences of people, situations and objects by representing them.

In recent years the work of early childhood practitioners in Reggio Emilia has caught the attention of the international early childhood community. As David Hawkins (1998) points out in an essay he calls, 'Remarks: Malaguzzi's Story, Other Stories', 'I think it is worth remembering a few of those other stories. Let me mention others. In the field of education, as in many others, good theory – I boldly say – has come mostly as a harvest, a reflection of successful practice. Harvested from past practice, theory in turn can, then, bring new practical guidance.'

In the UK, good practice in the mainstream emerged mainly through the influence of Friedrich Froebel from the late nineteenth century onwards. The Reggio Emilia work reiterates much of this, with its emphasis on encouraging young children to develop their creativity, imagination, and to explore and solve problems. Malaguzzi talks about the 'Hundred Languages of the Child' (Edwards, Gandini and Forman, 1998). Children are encouraged to develop their thinking through in-depth projects. These are a cooperative venture between practitioners and children. In the UK nursery tradition, this would be described as supporting and extending a child's individual interest. In England this is now almost impossible to achieve with the depth there used to be, because children often only spend one year in settings, and there are no children over the age of four years in many. In Reggio Emilia children stay for three years, from the age of three until they are six years old, and this makes a huge difference, as they keep their two teachers for three years. Artists work with the children.

However, something that brings a new dimension to the approach of helping children to learn in depth is the work done in small groups, rather than aiming this at an individual child. In practice, small-group work emerged in the early childhood practice of the nursery schools in the UK, because when one child becomes interested in something in depth, it tends to fascinate other children too. But the Reggio approach is more community based. It emerged when

Malaguzzi led a group of practitioners after the war in 1945, with a view to avoiding the pre-war traditional domination of the Roman Catholic Church in the education system, and encouraging a community of learners and a sharing of culture. There is a pedagogista who works with several schools and centres, reporting to the Director for the region's local government. The links between local government and the Reggio settings are therefore deep.

The emphasis on documentation is also a useful and thought-provoking aspect of the work in Reggio Emilia. Documentation gives children a concrete memory of their learning journey. These have always been called interest books in the UK context. Currently there is a surge of profile, social books or learning journey books, which are in this spirit. They provide the parents and community with information and encourage them to feel part of things. Settings in the UK now put more emphasis on using the walls and display cabinets in an expanded form of documentation. This is, as in Reggio, more of a community journey than the individual journey of a child. An aspect of documentation that has been taken forward in some UK projects, such as the 'Oxfordshire Creativity Project', or the 'Hundred Voices Project ', both part of the '5×5×5=creativity initiative', is the way documentation can help practitioners, artists and researchers to develop their work with children and the community.

It is important to remember that it is neither possible nor desirable to transplant a culture. But Reggio Emilia reiterates key messages of the work of great educators preceding it, and also expands that work in ways that are useful in taking forward practice in the UK today in relation to documentation, the need to reform the length of time children spend in their early childhood setting, to raise the school starting age, and to develop a more integrated system with schools and settings and local government, so that citizenship and trust is encouraged and made possible.

Offering children performances, stories, music and dance so that they are introduced to other people's ideas and representations

Much of the theatre, dance and music offered to children as performance for them is, at best, patronising and, at worst, undervalues their possibilities for sophisticated understanding and appreciation as developing symbol-users, who are attuned to their cultural and social contexts and communities. Children deserve the best in theatre, dance and music. Good children's theatre, dance, music and literature has layers of meaning, which fascinate adults as much as the children, such that everyone takes from the piece what holds meaning for them.

Conclusion

* Representation is a process in human development.
* It gives children and adults ways of keeping hold of important experiences through images and symbols.
* Images can be to do with what we hear, see, smell, taste and touch, or what we do in terms of movement.
* We use symbols to make one thing stand for another, usually in the absence of the person, object, place or event. Some symbols are very personal and idiosyncratic. These are understood only by the person using them and perhaps those close to them. Some symbols are shared conventions, arbitrary by nature, such as words, writing, music, dance, notation or algebra.
* The early childhood curriculum encourages children to:
    * be active learners;
    * make images;
    * develop symbols, both personal and shared conventions.
* Special objects or toys might become what Winnicott calls 'transitional objects', easing children into and out of situations involving separation from those they are close to, and at the same time encouraging the representational process to develop.
* The process of representation leads towards children (and adults) developing interests and hobbies in life. The biological path of development (our genetic programme) is constantly in touch with, is part of and is influenced by the socio-cultural path of our development. Consequently, even identical twins might develop different interests.
* The process of representation develops as a web or network involving:
    * the senses;
    * movement;
    * imitation;
    * making images – making symbols.
* The process of representation involves a sense of ownership by the child: young children representing their own experiences, their own ideas, feelings and relationships, and not those of others that are not part of their experience.

Communicating with and without words: the foundations of literacy

Non-verbal communication

Communication is central to being a human. Non-verbal communication never stops. Even when we are asleep we communicate to others whether we are restful, physically comfortable or dreaming. Non-verbal communication is the main way in which we communicate, through our facial expressions, body language movements and gestures, tone of voice, pauses and much else too. It is a background to living. Some estimates suggest that it forms 85 per cent of our communicating. Others suggest 75 per cent.

Babies

Work over many years by Colwyn Trevarthen (1993a, 1998; Malloch and Trevarthen, 2009) shows how babies communicate and 'speak' to those close to them in non-verbal ways. They move in synchrony with the voice of the parent or sibling in a dance-like fashion. They 'reply' when spoken to, provided that the person pauses long enough for them to make the reply and does not constantly 'talk at' the baby.

Children communicate with much-loved family pets

Animals, especially mammals, also communicate non-verbally. It is not only a feature of human living. Researchers working with the American Academy of Child and Adolescent Psychiatry suggest that:

> The strong emotional bond that develops between a pet and a child can also have a positive impact on the way a child is able to communicate. Children who have pets are more able to understand non-verbal communication as they derive signs of an animal's happiness from a wagging tail or stiff posture. Children apply these skills to their interactions with people and become better at working out what people's posture and facial expressions mean.
>
> (Crown, 2004: 16)

The example is given of Ben, aged seven years, who notices of his collie-cross dog, that 'when Tarka is confused, he does not meet my eyes, and he slouches. People do this too sometimes' (Crown, 2004: 16).

It is important to note that children need intimate, sustained, warm affectionate relationships with people (and perhaps with much-loved family pets), if they are to learn to read their own feelings, ideas and movements, and those

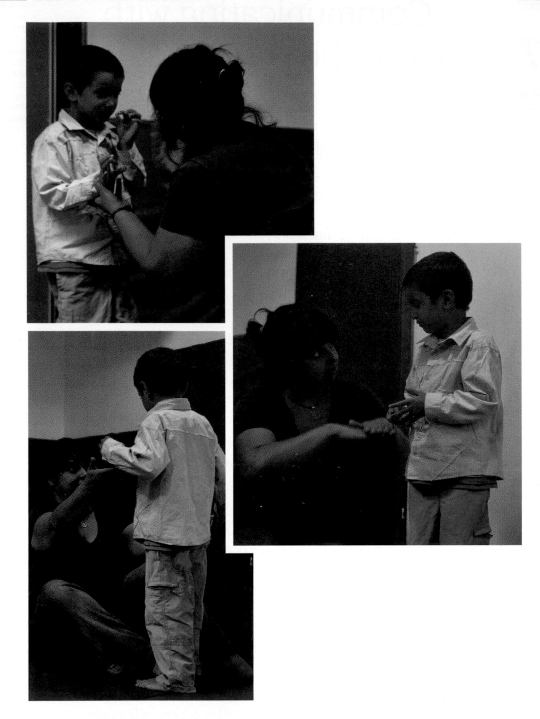

Figure 7.1: Eye contact and facial expressions help communication. This is why it is important to get down to the child's level. The boy is anxious at first, but the adult encourages him to join in, with non-verbal communication through her eye contact and body movements, and through quiet and encouraging conversation with him. He replies with nods rather than words.

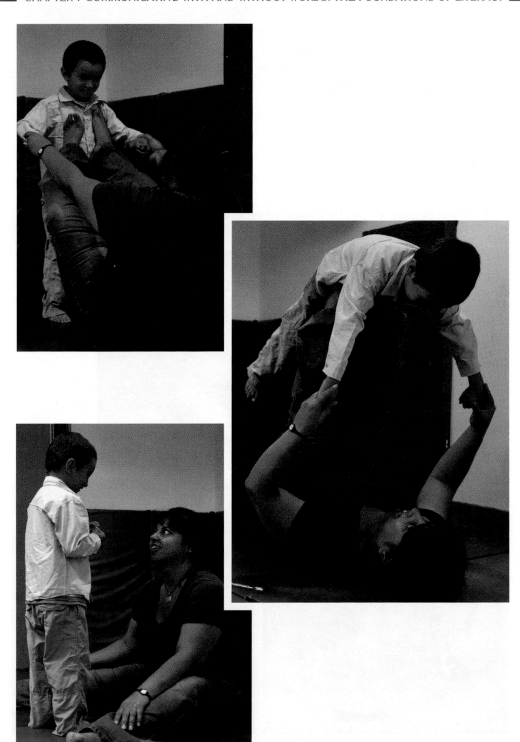

Figure 7.1: *Continued*

of others with sensitivity. Having animals in a group setting may, however, have the opposite impact to the one aimed for. Often, animals kept in early childhood settings lead miserable lives, with children handling them too roughly and without any bond or real relationship.

Non-verbal communication is central to many aspects of child development

In other parts of this book much has been said about the importance of non-verbal communication. Please see in particular Chapter 6 (representation), Chapter 8 on thinking about how others feel and think, Chapter 9 on people who matter to children, and Chapter 10 on diversity, inclusion and the equalities.

Figure 7.2: The adult is helping the boy to use the knife, giving him clear instructions, as well as plenty of eye contact and smiles to encourage him to feel confident and help him to develop the skill. Children learn best when they receive the right help at the right time in the right way.

Spoken or signed language

Spoken language is also about communication, communication with self and communication with others

It helps people to move from the here and now to the past, into the future and into alternative worlds. It uses agreed signs that evolve to fit the times and setting in which the language is used. It enables people to think and feel at an abstract level about ideas that are hypothetical and imaginary in effective, efficient, deep and moving ways. It involves talking and listening.

In western culture all four elements are important areas of language in the school setting and in life generally. To be illiterate sets people at a disadvantage.

To be unable to talk or listen cuts people off and brings loneliness and frustration along with the lack of opportunity to communicate with others. Language does not have to be oral. It can be 'talked' or 'listened to' in different ways. Some deaf and blind people talk and listen through touch. The language of the deaf has gained recognition as an official language: British Sign Language (BSL). This is not an oral language. It combines gesture, agreed and shared signs with finger spelling.

The work of researchers such as Mary Brennan (1978) and Judy Kegl (1997) has helped those who use oral language to appreciate that sign language has a syntax and has evolved just as any living language, has regional dialects and enables abstract thinking. It contains features shared by verbal languages. It facilitates thinking, feeling and communication. It allows those who understand it to construct shared meanings together. However, like some other languages in the world, it has no written form and so cannot be read.

Listening and talking

After the Sandinista Revolution of 1979 in Nicaragua, a group of deaf children came together for the first time when a school for deaf children was founded in Managua, joined by the researcher Judy Kegl (1997). When the children met in this special school they had only a few idiosyncratic and personal signs, as they had grown up isolated, as one deaf person living among a hearing community in their homes.

As they continued to meet, a natural development occurred. They began to develop a 'pidgin language', which was a basic language that gave them the means, for the first time in their lives, to share ideas and feelings, and to communicate with each other. The older children (teenagers) continued to use this language, but the younger children continued to develop it until what linguists call a 'creole language' emerged out of the pidgin language. This was a fully fledged sophisticated sign language, which was quite unique in the world, using grammar and a rich vocabulary.

Judy Kegl argues that humans are genetically and biological predisposed to develop grammatical language systems. These children did it – out of nothing! But, and this is important in looking at the way language develops, there are two socio-cultural aspects to her findings.

1. Both the basic pidgin language and the sophisticated creole language had taken in elements of gestures used in the Nicaraguan culture and transformed these in a more developed form into the vocabulary of the language.
2. When Judy Kegl visited deaf children in rural areas, living at home without contact with other deaf children, they used only primitive gestures and signs without any grammatical element. When she introduced the children to each other, and taught them the full creole form of the sign language, the younger children quickly took it up and became fluent.

In other words, biology alone is not enough. A language acquisition device (as proposed by Chomsky in the 1960s) needs the company of other people to be triggered to the full. We need other people because we are social animals. We need, literally, to participate with other people in our culture and language. It is not as simple as teaching children to talk. In this case, the younger children were teaching the teenagers and adults the creole, the more sophisticated form of the language.

Most of the time adults and children, through participating with each other in the language and the culture, will be teaching each other different things. It seems that Froebel's statement that we 'need to live with our children' still holds true today.

Bilingual children listening and talking

Marian Whitehead (2007: 15) points out that, in many countries of the world, such as Wales, Quebec, Belgium and South Africa, several languages are spoken officially. Where this is the case, there is a more positive attitude in society towards children who are multilingual. The result is that it is easier for children to learn several languages. She identifies four aspects of the complexity and achievements of children who are multilingual. Competence changes according to the language being spoken. If children switch from using their first language to the second, their vocabulary may be less, and they may not be able to read or write with the confidence shown in the first language. Very few children grow up as balanced bilinguals.

Second, she suggests that children use different languages with different people and when they are in different situations. They might mix two languages, but this could be by choice so that they can express and find the words for what they want to say, rather than any confusion.

Marian Whitehead (2007: 20) suggests that these so called 'mistakes' are in fact very successful strategies for language learning.

Third, children often speak but do not read or write in a language. Some languages are oral and do not have a written form. Last, when situations change, languages can be lost. A child might move to another community; a key person who spoke to them in a language might leave, or die. Some linguists take the view that when this happens the language becomes dormant and could be activated at a later time, rather than it becoming lost.

Children who are bilingual grow up more easily able to appreciate and value differences between people and cultures. This helps them to make sense of social situations. It is important that early childhood educators make every child feel that their language and culture is welcomed, valued, respected, acknowledged and visibly supported.

Children who speak three languages with entirely different roots, have a range of sounds and understandings that are, in every sense, mind-expanding. Examples would be the ability to speak Arabic, French and English; or Swahili, German and Italian; or Finnish, Danish and Xhosa. This, Marian Whitehead (2007: 20) points out, gives children the advantage of thinking about the system behind a language, so that they are well equipped for literacy learning.

Encouraging language

We learn to talk through talking. Children need to spend time with people who are sensitive to their needs and who encourage them. Often one child will 'translate' to an adult what another child means. Parents are also able to signal to early years workers about events and situations that will help the communication between them and the child. Similarly, early years workers can promote the parent/child relationship by telling parents what was done in school and inviting them in to show them.

> Three-year-old **RICHARD** was met each day from nursery class by his mother. The early years worker made a point of suggesting that, if parents were not in a rush, their child could show them round. In this way parents had an idea of the activities, models, paintings and so on in which their child was involved. Later, at home, when Richard referred to a dead worm, his mother did not have to puzzle over his meaning. She knew that he was studying newts in school and that worms were fed daily to them. When, in school, Richard talked about 'my yellow one', the teacher knew that he had a new teddy bear because his mother had mentioned it.

As children grow up they can be helped to become aware of the need to explain and fill in necessary information in order to bring meaning to those who were not present. Listening to stories, reading and writing facilitate this process. These are strong links with the ability to develop a sense of 'audience'.

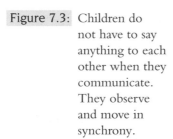

Figure 7.3: Children do not have to say anything to each other when they communicate. They observe and move in synchrony.

A group of seven-year-olds were going round a stately home. The guide wanted to talk about the ceramics. The teacher sensed that this held no interest for the class. She did know about some of the paintings and asked the children to look at a painting of a lady. She asked what **ZOE**, **MARK** and the picture had in common. The situation changed, from a monologue by the guide to suggestions from the children with the teacher acting as chairperson. Eventually, it was established that Zoe and Mark had both recently acquired baby sisters. The children wondered if that was the link. Had the lady just had a baby? In fact, the fine lady in the painting had founded a maternity hospital for the poor. The children asked about her, why she did this, who she was.

This teacher had taken the children into history and helped them to glimpse the social order of a different time from their own. The language introduced was rich but welcomed. The teacher had helped to establish a partnership by starting from something that the class found interesting and relevant. Her share of the partnership was achieved; it was to link up with a project on Victorian Britain, including the contrast between wealth and poverty, and the social order of the times.

Children need to have opportunities to initiate conversations in early childhood settings during activities and during group times. They also need individual and small-group times; for example, when involved in music, dance or story. In these settings they can interject and the adult can use these interjections to make the story meaningful at a deeper level.

'I've got one of these' may seem an egocentric response by four-year-old JASON to the story of Titch by Pat Hutchins. However, it tells the early years worker that Jason knows about a pinwheel. He explains how it goes round if you blow on it. He wants to abandon the story at this point and talk about his pinwheel instead. The practitioner can let him talk with her because it is a small group of three children. The other children bring in information about how the pinwheel works. When the early years worker has taken each child's initiations about the subject, she takes them back to the text. Jason often returns to this story, provided it is in the book corner. Old favourites are an important part of leading towards reading.

When adults are involved in discussions with small groups (two to four children) the advantages are that children are less likely to lose the focus of the conversation when it is not their turn to speak. They do not have to wait too long if they are bursting with a thought on the subject. It is also easier for the adult to draw children into the discussion, and to make use of the contextual backcloth of what children say. Even so, there are frequently times when adults need the help of other children to 'translate' or give the contextual clues needed for the conversation to flow and make sense to everyone participating.

Three-year-old LUCKDEEP sat down for story time when the teacher told the story of Mrs Wishy Washy and kept saying 'in there'. The teacher wanted to respond but did not understand. SANDEEP explained that Luckdeep wanted the teacher to put the scrubbing brush in the bowl to make soap bubbles. The shared socio-cultural context was not enough. It was necessary to negotiate a shared meaning, too. The practitioner then built the bubbles in to the story.

Iram Siraj–Blatchford and colleagues (EPPE, 2003) stress the importance of 'shared sustained conversations' with children around rich experiences with them.
    Children are active in their learning and need to be encouraged in this. Their active feelings affect their active thinking. One deep, powerful experience is better than many pedestrian ones.

Six-year-old **TOM**'s mouse died. He was very upset. A story about a mouse and his experiences in a cage, and how he runs away leaving his owner sad, contains in it some of Tom's grief. He loved the story. It evoked the memory of the feelings he had in ways that were comforting for him. Tom did not choose the story; his mother did, recognising the importance of the death of his mouse.

Adults need to choose books for children that help them to meet and extend both powerful and everyday experiences. Sometimes these will arise spontaneously, as with Jason and the pinwheel. Sometimes they need to be planned by the adult, as with Tom. Children relate their own experiences to those of others through books, shared activities and outings, provided that adults allow them to be active in the process. Sometimes the child initiates, sometimes the adult, but the child always needs to be active.

Figure 7.4: Children who are becoming sensitive communicators, helped by adults to become so, notice what other children need and they take care of each other. Here they take care of the girl's blockplay construction.

The importance of feelings

Margaret Meek (1985: 43) stresses the need to 'foreground the emotive' in this process. She sees emotion as an integrating force in children's experiences. As well as listening to stories and being helped to interact with the text, children produce nonsense rhymes and jokes that are a very important aspect of their being active in their language development.

Chukovsky (1963), and more recently Marian Whitehead (2007, 2009, 2010) and Goswami and Bryant (1990) all note the value of rhyming sounds as an important element in learning to read. Jeni Riley (1996: 28) emphasises the importance of adults capitalising on the way children naturally enjoy songs and rhythm.

Piaget sees playing with ideas and making jokes as the highest level of understanding. Helping children develop a sense of humour was one of the central aims of Chris Athey's project during 1972–77. Having fun with language, or with any area of knowledge, implies good understanding and can be used as a means of assessing what children know well.

Rearranging ideas and words is the basis of the creative process. Talking and listening, partnerships and being active in language development, lead in to literature. Peter McKellar (1957) defines the imagination as the rearrangement of past experience in new and fascinating ways.

The importance of making errors free from criticism – experimenting

Wells (1987: 18) argues for

> the value of errors, to learners as elicitors of helpful feedback and for teachers as a source of insight into the meanings that their pupils are making.

In talking, children are attempting actively to formulate the rules of language. They hypothesise for example, 'I hitted the ball'. If adults reply by extending, 'Oh, you hit the ball, did you?', they give the correct form without rejecting what the child said. This helps children to adjust their 'rules' for themselves. Direct correction of children's speech is ineffective and may create stress – for adults as well as children. Self-correction is an important strategy as children check for meaning. It also tells adults where children are in their development.

Writing

In order to put the development of writing into context, it is necessary to return to Chapter 6 on representation. Writing is an aspect of language, which is an aspect of representation.

Winnicott (1974) proposed the importance of the transitional object in the early development of representation. Baby Lion stood for the link between the mother and the child as well as the space between them when they were apart. Baby Lion was Ellen's first possession and creation.

Vygotsky, in agreement with Winnicott, goes further. He is quite clear that early representation leads directly to written language. He points out that gesture is of paramount importance: playthings and drawings initially acquire meaning supported by gesture. A pencil becomes a person. A book cannot become a person, but its dark green cover could allow it to be turned into a forest. Gradually, objects acquire a meaning independent of gesture. Make-believe, says Vygotsky (1978), is a major contributor to the development of written language. So is drawing.

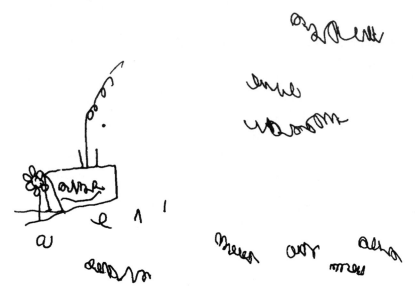

Figure 7.5: Drawing and writing together – zig zag schema.

Drawing and writing together – zig zag schema

Representation is one of the keys to writing. Vygotsky's thinking is very much in tune with that of Marie Clay (1975), whose work has been an important influence on research and thinking about early writing. She suggests that children need to construct their own writing system, a theory of their own that they can operate. They need to be allowed to experiment and develop their own theories.

Early writing must be unhindered by external demands for neat letter forms, proper spacing, writing on the line and conventional spelling

Ferreiro (1997; Ferreiro and Teberosky, 1983), building on the work of Vygotsky, and Dame Marie Clay argue that thinking about early writing has overemphasised the graphic shapes (the transcriptive aspects) and under emphasised composition. Handwriting, letter formation, legibility and speed have tended to be the main focus of adults helping young children to learn to write.

Like Vygotsky, Ferreiro and Teberosky believe that children first try to 'find the frontier that differentiates drawing from writing'. Initially, children begin to put letters into their pictures, but they suggest that the letters do not 'say' anything by themselves. There is only a vague relationship between letters and drawing.

> Adults have the key role of acknowledging and responding to a child's first attempts at writing and of knowing at what stage to intervene sensitively in order to develop writing skills. This is vital if a child is to develop the confidence to become a writer. It is therefore important that all staff are enabled to develop skills of observing children and of analyzing these observations with an understanding of both the curriculum content and a thorough knowledge of how children learn and develop.
>
> (Bunting, 2003b)

Six-year-old Raymond uses the R to represent himself, the D to represent his foster mother Daphne, and the H to represent his foster father Hywel. Some letters are easier to write than others. Prospective parents choosing names, please note! Curves, such as those in C and in J, with an open semi-circle, are more difficult.

Figure 7.6: Core and radical schema.

Capital letters are easier for children to write – so children usually select them for their first attempts at writing

Vygotsky, and the later work of Ferreiro and Teberosky, add support to Marie Clay. Children do not seem to be 'taught' capital letters by ignorant, tiresome parents, although practitioners often accuse innocent parents of this! Children probably use them, if Piaget is right, because they select patterns that they can draw easily. They use complete enclosures and trajectories, separate and in combination. This means that, broadly speaking, they tend to use capitals first, and the more difficult lower-case letters later.

Figure 7.7: Enclosure, trajectory and core and radial schemas.

Children are active problem-solvers as they try to encode their marks into writing

The alphabetic symbols used by children could well be the stepping stones towards conventional writing. I remember using a nail file to carve my name in capitals with painstaking care on the wooden mantelpiece. My mother tells me I was four years old.

Nigel Hall (in Hall and Martello, 1996: 98) writes:

> Just as they create non-conventional versions of spelling patterns, so they generate non-conventional rules for punctuation. Although their rules may be non-conventional … it is reasoning not guessing that is involved.

An inclusive approach to writing that embraces diversity

It is important to create learning environments indoors and outdoors that encourage writing. Putting notepads into the home area next to the telephone encourages children to write, for example. It is also important to embrace the diversity of the socio-cultural contexts of home literacy. Charmian Kenner (2000: 23) emphasises the importance of making literacy links between home and the early childhood setting that embrace principles of equality, inclusion and diversity. In the UK today many children have varied experiences of literacy that do not necessarily mirror the way literacy is approached in schools.

As young children begin to experiment with writing, for example shopping lists, in their play, seeing the writing of other children and adults, and seeing print in school, Ferreiro (1997) suggests they experience a conflict. Ferreiro, giving resonance to the findings of Judy Kegl on language development, suggests that learning to write is not entirely dependent on the external socio-cultural environment, but that there are also internal organisational mechanisms at work. She argues that children, as they learn to write, are learning about the nature of the link between oral and written representations. Jeni Riley (2006) reiterates the importance of this connection.

As children observe and write, there are conflicts to be resolved and experiments to be made in writing. For example, Ferreiro's research demonstrates how children find monosyllabic words a challenge, because they like to have between three and five characters in a cluster in order to feel that they have written a word. 'AMA' stands for Amanda, and matches the number of syllables in her name. 'BO +' stands for Ben, but does not match the number of syllables in his name. The children tend to put in a 'dummy' (extra marks), because of their minimum rule. They like to have three 'letters' to make a 'word'. For this reason, according to Ferreiro, children find longer words, with more syllables, such as 'dinosaur', with three syllables, or 'refrigerator', with five syllables, easier to tackle than 'boat', with only one syllable.

The importance of your own name

Again, the child's own name cannot be given too much emphasis. It may be the first 'fixed string', as Ferreiro and Teberosky (1983: 207) call it, that the child meaningfully encounters. It serves a useful purpose in causing internal conflict in the child between the number of letters and the number of sounds between the alphabetic and syllabic codes. Striving to resolve this conflict between letters and sounds takes the child into a new level of understanding of what is involved in writing. As children resolve the conflicts inherent in this, they gradually break the writing code. Ferreiro and Teberosky say (1983: 277):

> Let children write, even in a writing system different from the alphabetic one. We must let them write, not so [that] they invent their own idiosyncratic system, but so [that] they discover that their system is not the conventional one, and in this way find valid reasons to substitute their own hypotheses with our conventional ones.

It is a serious matter when children enter school at five years old, thinking that they do not know how to write their own names and believing that only by tracing and copying will they come to know.

> The distance between copy writing and children's spontaneous writing is as great as the distance between copy drawing and children's spontaneous drawing.
>
> (Ferreiro and Teberosky, 1983: 278)

If children entering school are seen as deficient in knowledge of the alphabetic code, and in dire need of swift initiation into it, the teaching of writing will be tackled by asking them to trace letters, copy sentences, correctly form their letters and, as soon as possible, by introducing punctuation, spelling and grammar.

The importance of adults who support and extend literacy learning

Ferreiro is not arguing that children should be left to themselves in learning to write. Like Weinburger (1996), Riley (2006) and Whitehead (2010) she suggests that children need support and help as they move into the role of writers. Riley stresses the importance of children working out letter/sound relationships as part of this. Donald Graves (1983) works on the principle that the adult's role is to help children 'find their own voice' in writing. As an adult writer of any book, I find that it is very important to encourage children to write with confidence.

Ferreiro (1997), Clay (1975, 1992) and Miller (1997) suggest that, at an early age, in the first five years, children can be truly educated in the writing process. There is a desire in this approach to build on what the child already knows and, with adult and peer group help, progress from there. The two-year-old who draws and make-believes is perhaps already sharing creations with the significant people in his or her life, and this is the basis of writing.

Family literacy

Colin Harrison (1996: 25) gives a three-part definition of family literacy:

1. the spontaneous family literacy activities;
2. inter-generational projects to improve the literacy levels of both parents and children;
3. support or intervention programmes encouraging children's literacy development within the family.

Denny Taylor (1983: 87) sees the family as the base of literacy: 'Literacy is part of the very fabric of family life' (we ought perhaps to add 'in some cultures'). Denny Taylor also believes that 'literacy can be a barrier between home and school, and a contrivance of familial dissent' (1983: 87).

> ANDREW would not do word and picture matching with his mother. Instead, he made the cards intended for this purpose into an eagle, which he cherished. His mother sensibly gave up!

The damaging impact of a narrow skills approach to early literacy

Kathy Goouch (in Goouch and Lambirth, 2007) interviewed a group of highly educated parents whose children were about to begin reception class in English primary schools. She found that parents were anxious that their children should continue to enjoy books and the writing efforts they made in their families.

They did not want this to be spoilt through pressure. They were unaware of recent developments towards a phonics first approach, and were nervous about the possible harmful effects of an over-emphasis on skills work in the early years of education.

The way that the family's approach meets the school's approach to literacy is a very important consideration in working with young children, but the way that the child interacts with his or her own family in relation to literacy is also important. Personalities are involved, as well as the education style of the parents, and they influence the literacy experiences of the children within the home. From the beginning, the child is both active and reactive to his or her own family's literate experiences and presentations of them.

Parents find that each of their children differs in her or his responses to 'writing'. At three years, HANNAH would 'write' in zig-zagging cursive a shopping list whenever her mother did so. She loved to sign greetings cards with a capital H. She loved stories, often demanding them during the day, as well as expecting as many as possible at bedtime.

At three years, WILLIAM, who was the second child from the same family, would just about concentrate for a bedtime story. Mother had to work hard to keep his concentration, whether he chose the stories or whether she did. However, he loved to lie in bed and listen to his five and a half year old sister read to him until he fell asleep. This also helped her reading to develop, of course! At four years, William began to enjoy his bedtime story with mother, often choosing the same one several nights in a row, for example *The Tale of Mr Jeremy Fisher* by Beatrix Potter. He would not tolerate any deviation from the text, which he knew inside-out. He showed no interest in writing, except for the W of his name with which he would sign the occasional drawing.

At four and a half years, Hannah was reading a few words, such as 'Hannah' and 'Mummy', and writing all the time. By five years, she had 'cracked' the alphabetic code. At four and a half years, William began writing his name frequently, and then cutting it out and sticking it on to models he had made. By five and a half years, he had cracked the alphabetic code, and was always asking his mother for just one more episode of a story. He showed no desire to write, except for his name, but constantly wanted his mother to write notes as reminders to do things.

Practitioners need to tune in to the child's family literacy

Shirley Brice Heath (1983), among others, has stressed the importance of the teacher tuning in to the child's family. What is the family's understanding of and approach to literacy? To bedtime stories?

Denny Taylor (1983: 54) shows us how families 'salute and hurt' each other through print. Seven-year-old Hannah writes her mother a note: 'I'm terribly sorry about the nail varnish remover.' Mother writes to father, 'You are late. Supper burnt. Serves you right.'

Functional literacy at home

Hall and Robinson (2003) stress that the gains children make through family literacy programmes are difficult if not impossible to measure reliably until children reach the age of 9 or 10 years. They emphasise the importance of home visits, and how parents appreciate help with how to support their child's reading at home. It emerges that parents do not naturally or automatically know how children are helped towards literacy just because they are parents. Children learn about the multiplicity of literate activities as they participate in different social events (for example, birthday cards, shopping lists, bills). In fact, children often engage in writing activities of which the parent is unaware. Scraps of paper might exist all over the house, with phone messages, reminders, stories and so on written on them, which are purposeful and functional. The home is where children are introduced to functional literacy. Its importance cannot be over-emphasised. This is supported by the EPPE research (DfES, 2003).

There is a potential problem if those working with young children from outside the family setting, whether in the school setting, the day nursery or during home visits, attempt to tell parents what they should do. This is a partnership on professional terms. An equal partnership demands a more reciprocal approach to the relationship (Athey, 1990; Bruce, 2004).

Children need to see adults 'writing for real'

It is important to give children experiences that build on those of their home life. A child might have been to the corner shop, the market or the supermarket. Any of these experiences can be added to or taken further. Another consideration is the need for children to imitate. Seeing adults involved in functional writing, at the bank, making shopping lists with the children and writing notes for the milkman is important in this respect. Writing needs to be demonstrated in a functional and purposeful way, so that children can select what they will represent or write about.

A student took in plenty of found materials for the three- to four-year-olds in the nursery school. She set them out attractively, made herself very available by sitting at the table, and the children flocked to make models. John experimented with glue, covering the box! Segun had a plan to make a can. He wanted to 'do writing' on the can of food he made. No two models were the same, and not all were representational. The student was not imposing her theme of 'shape' on this group of children, although there was plenty of skilful 'shape' talk popped in at appropriate moments, in sensitive ways. Donald Graves might say that the student was helping the children to find their own voice, rather than to echo the thoughts of the adult, which would be a narrow and passive response, and soon becomes boring.

However, if children are to find their own voice they need a great deal of support and encouragement from adults, since to do this is much harder than copying. If they are to reach satisfaction and a sense of fulfilment, they need to be helped through the inevitable struggles involved in any worthwhile activity.

Being there at the right moment to hold the glue pot still, to stretch out the sticky tape for it to be cut by the child, to hear the story the child has woven around the model and to support them in their writing on the model are all actions by adults that are part of encouraging representation and have implications for early writing. In early writing work, representation is a key factor.

In attempting to do this, it has been necessary to refer back to previous chapters. And it is also necessary to value the family's contribution. Children need a wealth of first-hand experiences to make learning to write meaningful, and to set it in a functional and purposeful context.

The importance of play scenarios

Representation through writing during play is important in all its facets, in stories, dance, songs, home corners, doll's houses, construction toys, paints, models and drawings. Among all this, children can be encouraged to 'write', in the classroom post office, restaurant, hairdresser, bank, and so on. 'Real writing' is only the culmination of a long process towards it.

Early dramatic play helps children to explore roles and themes, beginnings, endings, transitions, all of which are vital to the writing process.

> At Tachbrook Nursery School staff work deliberately to develop children's experience of and capacity for sustained imaginative play throughout the whole of the four to six terms that individual children attend the nursery school. The emphasis is on allowing the story play to develop over significant stretches of time, often over a term and sometimes for much longer.
>
> (Jane Bunting, interview with Tess Robson, 2003)

The importance of drawings

When a child does four apparently identical drawings, they may be the equivalent of attempts to revise and redraft in the writing process.

> Two children, William and Tom, discuss a drawing. Both are four years old. 'Why is its mouth there?' 'It's hungry, silly. That's its tongue, going like that.' He sticks out his tongue. They break into laughter.

Figure 7.8: The adult and toddler are sharing a book (A). This is more than talking together. Much of their communication with each other is non-verbal. They are joined by other children (B) and the adult looks at each of them (C), sitting at their eye level, so that all the children engage with the story.

Frank Smith (1983) believes that, at first, representational work is the child's creation, to be admired but not submitted like a manuscript to be scrutinised and criticised. He is in agreement with Winnicott in this. The creation belongs to the child. No one else can presume to alter it in any way. Vygotsky says that the willingness to take criticism, to submit a manuscript for the scrutiny of others, emerges from the social relationship formed with the 'interested person', who is invited by the child to share in and work on the creation.

Just as there needs to be a truly reciprocal relationship between parents and professionals, so there needs to be a reciprocal relationship between a child and adults who will manage to extend development in an educative way. Joan Tamburrini (1982) sees this informal teaching as the strength of early childhood education. Teaching does not have to be direct and formal to be 'teaching'. Indirect teaching is just as powerful, and often more powerful when working with young children and their families.

Reading

The importance of being read to cannot be over-emphasised

Shirley Brice Heath (1983), Henrietta Dombey (1983), Caroline Fox (1983), Marian Whitehead (2010), to name a few, are in complete agreement about the importance of reading to and not at young children. Older brothers and sisters also make an important contribution when they do this, as do the partnerships when children in Year 6 read to younger children.

The bedtime story is one important way in which, in a one-to-one situation, an adult can give meaning to the text. Dorothy Butler (1980) stresses that babies appreciate books. This has been taken up with the SureStart 'Books for babies' initiatives in England. By looking at books in this intimate and individually sensitive way, adults can take up children's initiatives, giving and extending the meaning in them. Children begin to meet different worlds with the adult as translator (Geekie and Raban, 1993; Whitehead, 2010).

The importance of song, dance and story in interpreting texts

Children from four to seven years of age watched a puppet show of Handa's Surprise. This shared experience was important in enabling children to grasp what is involved in formal book and story language. Pictures, dancers, puppets and songs help children to relate to formal book language. It is of central importance that children experience stories of their culture and its roots.

Knowing a story well – the old favourites – helps children to predict when they read. Reading is largely prediction. Children need to understand about syntax semantics and grapho-phonic aspects of texts in order to read. Their own knowledge of language, the way they have 'cracked the language code', will enable them to tackle syntax in a text. Children who are bilingual develop understanding of the way language works because teasing out differences across languages is part of their lived experience. Being aware in this way is called having metalinguistic knowledge (Pafford, personal communication). Having core texts selected by the staff, and favourite texts that emerge from the children responding to literature from home and other settings, supports prediction through familiar texts.

Listening to stories with a rich variety of texts helps children to learn about words and sentence structures in book language. The interpretations children have about meanings, the way they bring their own experiences to bear, enables this process. The more help they have had in using language with others in a meaningful way, and in using understanding of book language and its ability to create imaginative ideas in what Margaret Meek calls 'possible worlds', the better.

Phonological awareness

When children learn to read and write, they are on a journey that requires many things to be in place before they learn how to map sounds on to letters. Phonological awareness is about becoming aware of the sounds of the language, and being able to hear and manipulate the way these fall into syllables and rhyming chunks (Bruce and Spratt 2011: Chapter 9).

There are three phonological grain sizes, according to Goswami (2007). These are syllables, rhyming chunks and phonemes. 'Breakfast' has two syllables. Examples of a rhyming chunk are 'money' and 'honey'. These can be learned quite naturally by children across the world it seems. The third grain is phonemic awareness, and it is about the smallest sounds in the word: 't-ea'. Research suggests that children develop these three phonological grain sizes in that order. Children do not seem to develop phonemic awareness without direct teaching (Goswami, in Goouch and Lambirth, 2007).

Some languages are phonologically consistent, such as Welsh, Finnish and Italian. Some languages are consistent in the written form. Italian is an example. It is therefore no surprise that Maria Montessori chose to teach children to read using synthetic phonics as the central part of her method. It makes sense for Italian-speaking children. In Italian there is almost a 1:1 correspondence when mapping sounds on to letters.

Syllables

Children enjoy finding the syllables in their own names. Jack has one syllable, but Sarah has two. Clapping hands helps.

Rhyming chunks and families of words

Children find it easier to understand print when there are rhyming chunks. This links with introducing children to families of words.

'Going', 'knowing', 'sewing', 'blowing' and 'doing' are all 'ing' words.
'Hat', 'bat', 'cat' and 'sat', are all 'at' words.

Children vary in the order in which they establish these connections and understandings. This is why it is important to build observations and assess each child individually. Tuning in to each child's needs is the joy of being an early years practitioner.

Phonemes

These are the smallest sounds in the language. 'C–a–t' has three. Children seem to explore and learn about syllables and rhyming chunks quite naturally if they are in a supportive environment with people who help them. They need to be directly taught to understand phonemes, but as Bruce and Spratt emphasise (2011), this does not mean sitting them in large groups to be taught by rote. Singing and dancing traditional rhymes, chants and stories with discussion of the phonemes in context works well. There was a 14 per cent improvement (compared with a national improvement of 8 per cent) in the Communication, Language and Literacy scores at the end of the reception class in the Local Authority (Bruce and Spratt, 2011) using this carefully thought-through sequence of finger rhymes, action songs, nursery rhymes and poetry cards.

Mapping sounds on to letters – the alphabetic principle

Poetry cards (Bruce and Spratt, 2011) are invaluable in helping children to move from phonemic awareness to mapping those sounds on to letters. When children sing traditional nursery rhymes and other songs, they begin to hear the differences in the sounds. Adults can support them in this. But 'red' and 'bread' don't look the same when written down in English. It helps children if the first chunks of text have some consistency, and poetry cards provide this if they are carefully chosen. Marian Whitehead sees these as manageable chunks of text. Bruce and Spratt (2011) have developed a sequence of synthetic phonics learning, based on the biological sequence of speech sounds (as advised by speech and language therapists), phonemic awareness through song and traditional rhymes, and poetry cards giving children the support they need in mapping sounds on to letters and a growing understanding of the alphabetic principle. They support alliteration and rhyme, as well as the blending and segmenting of sounds.

It is important to note that the Scale Point Study (based on Local Authority results across England of the Early Years Foundation Stage Profile, 2008), showed that the high level of competence in children's use of phonics in spelling and their ability to write sentences with punctuation at five years of age was not vital for attaining a Level 3 at the end of Key Stage 1 in the English system. Just over half the children who attained a Level 3 in writing had gained these points.

English is one of the most irregular languages in the world. It is not consistent in the way it sounds or how it is written down. Seeing the word 'read' in isolation is a good example. According to the context, it will sound different; for example, 'Would you like me to read you a story?' or 'Have I already read this to you?' This is why asking children to read words out of context is of doubtful use. There is no sense in making learning to read more difficult than it needs to be (Bruce and Spratt, 2011), especially with an irregular language like English (Goswami, in Goouch and Lambirth, 2007).

Connecting the text and how it sounds when read out loud – listening posts

Putting stories on to cassettes, and encouraging children to listen to them through headsets while following in the book, is an activity often referred to as 'Listening Post'. This type of work gives further variety and helps the auditory aspect of reading. These are some of the ways in which children can be helped to move from picture books to reading the text, both at home, in early childhood settings and later in school. The multi-cultural aspects are, as for learning to write, crucial in learning to read. Children need to connect with texts, and there is now recognition of this in developing simple stories and texts that engage children. Many of these are translated into different languages, so that they are accessible core texts for a diverse range of children, and yet offer a shared narrative. Having shared stories is part of being in a community and feeling that you belong.

Marian Whitehead (2002) believes that effective reading teachers help beginners to draw on what they know about reading, and to use this in a wide range of strategies. These include semantic, syntactic, grapho-phonic, phonological awareness and bibliographic conventions, such as 'Where do I start on the page?' Taking all this into account, it is no surprise to suggest that by the time children reach the stage of 'real' reading and 'real' writing, they are already a considerable way along the route to literacy.

The best early start to literacy

* We need to nurture non-verbal communication with sensitivity, in alignment with spoken or signed language or, even better, languages.
* Children need dance, music, rhythm, rhyme and song together with poetry and stories with which they can feel a connection, become involved, feel included and participate.
* They need to be read to, sung, danced and storied with.
* They need to see their families and those they spend time with writing for reasons and purpose. They need to understand the functions of reading and writing in daily life, for information and for pleasure.

* They need to share texts in the intimacy of the bedtime story traditions, very individually and sensitively. They need to discuss stories and what moves them, stirs them, scares them, makes them feel comfortable.

* They need to discuss and explore how texts work, and their mechanics and components in embedded contexts. What is a letter? How does it sound in this context? How does this word work in this sentence? Where do I begin to decode this (break it down)? Where do I begin to encode it (build it up)?

* Unless communication, spoken and unspoken, helps children to become attuned to self, others, situations and stories, with plenty of talk around issues, then reading and writing will not develop richly. They will develop dutifully, which is not the same. Print-rich environments energise and give children freedom to explore print in ways that turn them into bookworms and keen writers – for life.

Learning how you and other people feel and think

8

Thinking about other people

Catching feelings and showing sympathy to someone are important in the process of developing empathy. Recognising how someone else feels and thinks, and understanding that this may be different from how you feel, is the key to developing empathy.

However, being able to read how other people feel and think develops out of the ability to know yourself, and to recognise and identify how you feel and think (Damasio, 2004; Gerhardt, 2004).

At a few months of age a baby will cry in sympathy with another child, as if recognising that someone is crying. By 15 months or so, toddlers will often comfort a brother or sister, friend or a loved adult in the way they would like to be comforted themselves, perhaps with a kiss or by bringing a special toy (Dunn, 1991). This ability to separate from self, at first caring for others as you would like to be cared for (sympathy) and gradually caring for others by recognising that they may have different feelings and thoughts and needs, is crucial for the development of spiritual, social and moral behaviour and well-being. In this chapter these important aspects of human development are given high focus.

Knowing you are a separate person, but knowing you can imitate or be imitated by someone else fascinates young children.

Thoughtful feelings

Feelings, Damasio (2004: 28) suggests, are our most private property. Emotions are more public, showing in our body reactions. They are the bedrock of our minds, but they are 'preludes to our feelings'.

Both the emotions and our feelings are basic mechanisms of life regulation, but feelings operate at a higher level. In earlier chapters we looked at Damasio's 'nesting principle'. Raw emotions are the simpler structures nesting within more complex and thoughtful feelings.

> Emotions are built from simple reactions that easily promote the survival of an organism and this could easily prevail in evolution.
>
> (Damasio, 2004: 30)

Key elements in learning how others feel and think

* Judy Dunn (1988, 1991) and Sue Gerhardt (2004) place great emphasis on the importance of helping children to recognise how they feel and think. **Knowing yourself** and reading yourself as you go through different experiences and relationships is of central importance.

* Children are helped when they are encouraged to **discuss and reflect on situations and events,** and to identify how they felt or thought, what went wrong and what they might do in a similar situation next time. Interestingly, this approach was central to Froebel's philosophy. Although the current emphasis in the literature is to support children in awareness of their feelings, and to encourage them to express these in relation to others, in the 1980s the emphasis was on metacognition and being aware of your own thinking, building on Piaget's work on intellectual egocentricity.

* Judy Dunn stresses the importance of **learning through and with brothers, sisters and close friends** in small groups in home settings. The **quarrels and shared good times** all contribute to the way children begin to learn how others feel and think. Children need to spend sustained time with the same children, ideally in mixed-age family groups, so that they learn to 'read' each other and tune in to how the others might react, feel and think. Seeing how others react to what people do is a crucial element.

* Children find it **easier to recognise the feelings of others than the way those people think,** but only if they are supported in reflecting on and analysing events and situations (see Bruce, 2004).

* Sue Gerhardt stresses the **role of the adult in helping children to identify and name their feelings,** tuning in to first the baby and then the young child's constantly changing emotional states. Babies and toddlers need enormous support in moving back to their 'comfort zone' once it has been wobbled or disturbed. This can be done

  by entering a baby's state with him, engaging him with a loud mirroring voice, gradually leading the way towards calm by toning her voice down and taking him with her to a calmer state.

  (Gerhardt, 2004: 23)

* Well-attached babies with parents who are well attuned to them (Stern, 2002) develop empathy for others more easily, **having experienced sustained loving care,** and developed a strong, embodied sense of self.

* However, Goleman points out that empathy is not all. Some children can empathise but because they have endured sustained emotional abuse, they 'become hyper-alert to the emotions of those around them, in what amounts to a post-traumatic vigilance to cues that have signalled threat'

(Goleman, 1996: 103). These children tend to become adults who are emotionally mercurial.

❋ **Good relationships are about constantly seeking balance between tuning in to your own feelings and thoughts, while reading and tuning in to the feelings and thoughts of others. The coordination of the two, self and others, is the key.**

The girl watches her friend build with the blocks, and is sensitive to her anxiety, keeping a good distance from her construction so as not to crowd her. The boy also respects her space, empathising with her situation.

Thinking of other people slips when a child is tired, with strangers, hungry, in a bad mood, in the company of those who are uncaring or unkind, or is herded in large groups. According to Celia Kitzinger (1997), this is probably the case for adults as well as children.

These issues have significance everywhere in the world, although in some countries the rights of and respect for the individual assume greater importance than those of the group as a whole, or vice versa. This has led to a debate on the issues surrounding human rights at international gatherings, the problems of market forces and individual greed, or the neglect of the needs of individuals in the cause of the state's needs.

Until recently, it was thought that young children were unable to put themselves into the position of someone else to any great extent. The influence of Jean Piaget's work (1968) led early childhood practitioners to see children under five years as 'intellectually egocentric'. This does not mean selfish.

Practitioners were trained to become skilled in diverting children, rather than attempting what was considered to be impossible – that is, trying to get the child to look at a situation from another child's point of view. As we have seen in the previous part of this chapter, with new research evidence things are more complex than Piaget suggested.

Four-year-old **WALLY** had been unhappy when settling into school himself. When he saw that three-year-old Peter was about to cry on his first day, he took Peter by the hand and cuddled him. He knew what it was like to be 'new' and could empathise.

Six-year-old **VICKY** and three-year-old **MARK** were eating ice cream. Vicky dropped hers and cried. Mark offered her some of his. He recognised the 'tragedy', as it seemed to him, of dropping an ice cream, as it had happened to him previously.

> TAMSIN (four years) was prone to frequent temper tantrums. She threw herself down and began punching the floor. MEGAN and PAUL came over, sank on their knees next to her and Megan said, 'I'm here for you, Tamsin.' They had seen Tamsin's tantrums given firm but compassionate attention by staff in the day nursery, and showed her respect. Tamsin looked up, took their hands and sank on the floor, calmed by feeling cared for.

Learning from everyday situations

Margaret Donaldson (1978) reminds us that children are able to perform at a higher level in a meaningful context. Piaget's tests presented children with formal tasks that were not in such a context. Margaret Donaldson distinguishes between:

* disembedded tasks (that is, abstract tasks, not performed in a realistic situation); and
* embedded tasks, which confront children in everyday, spontaneous events and situations.

The examples of Wally, Mark and Tamsin, quoted above, are embedded in meaning and so the children could relate to the situations.

> The teacher in a class of six-year-olds planned a cookery lesson. The children were to make baked apples in groups of six. They made one for themselves and one extra each to give as a present. JOANNA said that she wanted one for her brother and one for her mother. She, the teacher and the other children discussed the fairness of this – and eventually it was decided that she would have to cut up and divide the two apples when she got home. The teacher helped her to think of others, to see the unfair implications of giving her extra apples, and to become involved in the mathematics of division. She was helping her to consider others, justice and mathematics, all in a meaningful embedded context and yet moving slightly away from the immediate towards the disembedded context.

The current practice of showing children sets of disembedded photographs of facial expressions and asking them about feelings gleaned from the facial expressions of those in the photographs is the equivalent of using disembedded flashcards with words in isolation from literary texts, in order to teach reading. Children respond readily to literature through the meaning and context of words. Words or feelings in isolation from where they belong, in situations and stories and real life, are of little use in helping children to become bookworms or empathetic people in any real and lasting way.

Well-being

Moral development, which involves respecting and valuing others, emerges out of situations where children have sufficient sense of their own well-being to feel they can both give as well as take what they need in a relationship (Laevers, 1994). Children, or adults, who feel bad about themselves, are less likely to be highly developed morally as they will not so easily be able to move beyond their own needs to respecting and valuing those of other people.

Children need variety in the ways in which they mix with other children. Children need to work with children older and younger, more and less advanced, as well as children operating at the same level. This applies to both partnership and group situations. Partnerships can involve older and younger children, more and less advanced or children of the same age or stage. The following example shows partnership between two children at different points in their learning.

> Five-year-old **HANNAH** reads each night to three-year-old **WILLIAM**. The books he enjoys are at the level she can read 'approximately', from her knowledge of the story and the picture clues. She is thinking of stories that he enjoys, but she is gaining satisfaction from the giving by using her latest learning in a meaningful setting.

In batting a ball to a partner, or skipping together, each has to think of the other and get into the right positions, or the game will not be possible

What did I do? Why did you react like that?

Also, during this time, Judy Dunn shows how children, young though they are, begin sorting out what they are allowed to do. They begin to predict what people would disapprove of. Adults might well disapprove of kicking when you do not get what you want. A brother or sister might react strongly if you take a toy away. Young children need to explore and to discover what happens when they hurt other people, help other people or show care for other people. Judy Dunn's research suggests that families help children to tease out moral issues, where quarrels are followed by discussions of what went wrong and how to make things go better next time. She found that even before children can talk they benefit from learning about situations that make them angry, excited or joyous. The cause-and-effect relationship seems to be crucial. Before children can speak they know what makes people angry, and how people might react. It is initially through their relationships within the family that children learn to be caring of those they love.

Figure 8.1: An adult and a child are using the shuttlecock and bat together. They are thinking of each other, and which is the right position to make the rally a good and sustained one.

Figure 8.1: *Continued*

Identifying different emotions

Knowing about anger, love, jealousy, disgust, pride, humiliation and shame, disappointment, and so on, and how to deal with each, is an important contribution to moral development. Goleman (1996) and Gerhardt (2004) suggest that it is also fundamental for emotional health. Once there can be more discussion, this helps reflection and analysis around issues where children are not allowed to do something, share sadness and joy together, or play with other children.

Six-year-old **JENNY** asked for another pancake but there were none left. She was angry. Her mother reminded her that she had eaten two and that there were no more eggs. She said she understood that she felt disappointed, acknowledging her feelings rather than suppressing them. Goleman (1996) and Gerhardt (2004) stress the importance of allowing children to feel how they feel but helping them to deal with their feelings appropriately.

Negotiating with (not manipulating) people

Children in intimate settings, such as the family, learn to negotiate with other people rather than to manipulate them. Negotiation is part of moral development in that it respects other people. The process of manipulation of other people means grabbing for oneself, and indicates low self-esteem and lack of well-being in the child. It is, of course, normal to experience moments like this, but when adults help children to move on from these, moral development grows.

Four-year-olds **ALISTAIR** and **STUART** made a tune out of circles stuck on stave lines on a board. It was a monotone. The teacher sang it for them, and moved away. Stuart changed it so that it went up at the end, but Alistair did not want to change it. He tried to put the note down again, but Stuart grabbed it and ran off. Alistair gave chase; he was furious. Stuart's mother, who was helping in the classroom, said, 'Give him back his tune, Stuart.'

It was suggested by the teacher that Stuart should start another row underneath Alistair's, going up at the end. She then played this on the xylophone, Alistair played his row and Stuart played his. Here the negotiation broke down and the partnership required adult help. Neither child could decentre without help. The adult could have made Stuart apologise to Alistair, but preferred to give the message that it is more satisfying and produces better results to cooperate rather than fight.

Six-year-olds **TOM** and **WILLIAM** were in the garden together. Both are particularly interested in natural science and this had been the basis of a friendship since the age of three years. They found a crusader spider and made an assault course for it. They were delighted when it climbed up a pole and along a string they had rigged up. William tried to help it to realise there was another pole for it to climb down. He gently touched it, but the spider bit him. He was interested in this, as there had been discussion in his family for years about whether spiders did bite people. Both boys chatted constantly. 'Let's put a dead fly out for him to eat, then he'll come.' 'No it's got to be in a web.' 'Does he have a web or is he a pouncer?' 'What's a pouncer?' 'He hides and then pounces.' 'Oh!' There was a lot of negotiating.

The knowing–doing gap

It is very unusual for someone to give their life's work over to fighting a cause involving a moral principle. In the main, from adolescence to adulthood, people take on the socially expected conventions of their culture. It is only outstanding people, such as Nelson Mandela, who go beyond convention to take a moral stand. In other words, most people are more influenced by what other people do than they are by their conscience. It is therefore no good to expect children to know right from wrong, if they consistently see adults doing wrong. There needs to be a strong link between inner moral values and outer moral conduct. The expression 'do as I say, not as I do' is important where moral development is concerned.

MATTHEW (three and a half years) and his baby sister went with his parents to supper at the house of some friends. He was used to sleeping at other houses and happily went to bed upstairs. His father asked him to call out if the newly born baby started to cry. He agreed. A few minutes later he appeared downstairs crying and saying 'I don't want to.' His parents did not know what he meant, but it emerged that he did not want to tell the adults if the baby cried. He was happy to sleep upstairs, but did not want to think about the baby.

The parents reassured him and he was asleep in five minutes. His mother said that at home he took pride in telling her when the baby had woken up, in order to help her. He was tired and in a different setting, but the adults were sensitive to him.

Four-year-old PETER had a friend to tea and his mother joined them. There were soon only two scones left and Peter assumed that he and his friend would have them. His mother made no comment. Peter was not being helped to think about the problem of three people and only two scones. In a sense, his mother was holding back his social, spiritual and moral development by not raising this.

Good intentions and how others respond to them

Piaget found that children in middle childhood (approximately 8 to 12 years of age) were very concerned with what someone's intention was. If a child broke a cup by mistake when trying to clear the table, a younger child, for example a five-year-old, would say the helper was 'naughty' because the cup was broken, whereas an older child would understand that the intention was really to help and that breaking the cup was an accident.

In the early childhood years, it is therefore important that adults help children to tease out the importance of 'intention' as well as 'outcome'. This erodes the expression 'the end justifies the means'.

> HAYLEY (six years) went to fetch the pudding from the fridge to help her mother. She spilt custard in the fridge and left a trail of custard across the floor, and spilt it on her shoes and clothes. STACEY (three and a half years) said, 'You're naughty. You made a mess.' Stacey does not yet see that intention matters as much as outcome. Their mother said, 'Hayley was trying to help. She didn't mean to spill the custard.' Motive is as important as results, and motives involve feelings as much as ideas. Hayley's mother tried to keep alive her feeling of helpfulness by emphasising it, rather than the mess. Undermining a desire to help damages a child's long-term moral and social development.

Never call a child naughty – it widens the knowing–doing gap

It is probably best for adults never to call a child 'naughty'. Almost every juvenile delinquent has very low self-esteem. Feeling bad about yourself holds back social, emotional, spiritual and moral development. All of these are closely interwoven.

> Seven-year-old ANTHONY purposefully scratched a mark on a wooden table. The practitioner told him that he must not spoil the table in that way. He was crestfallen. So that he did not feel that she had rejected him, but only what he had done, she praised him when he picked a toy up that might have got crushed on the floor. She was firmly operating on the principle that there should be respect for property in the classroom in a meaningful context for Anthony. The practitioner pointed out that she had cared about the table being spoiled and she was glad that he cared about the toy being crushed. In this way she linked the two events.

Erikson (1963), through his eight stages of development, emphasised that through a basic sense of trust in the first year, self-esteem emerges in the second. If toddlers are constantly told that they are naughty, this soon withers.

The quality of early relationships is important.

* Intention needs plenty of discussion. Words such as 'meant to' and 'accidentally', 'on purpose' and 'mistake' would be part of the discussion.
* Being sorry about what has happened involves looking at a situation from another point of view, someone else's point of view. A child who can do this can be helped to try to make the situation better.

By helping to clear up the spilt custard some four-year-olds can think in the empathetic way, which leads to this kind of respect and sensitivity towards others. Hayley is not being blamed or made to feel guilt-ridden or ashamed. She feels sorry this happened, can see why it is upsetting to others but knows that her mother realises that it was unintentional and is doing what she can to make it better. Hayley's sense of well-being is not undermined. When a child intends 'wrong', for example by spilling custard on purpose, there can be discussion about it. 'I am sorry you did that. I don't like it when you make a mess on purpose.' In other words the adult is not rejecting the child, but what he or she did. The message is not:

* you are bad;
* I don't like you any more;
* you are naughty.

The message is:

* I don't like what you did;
* but you did try to clear it up;
* I still love you, unconditionally, whatever you do.

Resonances between toddlers and teenagers

There are strong links between the early childhood years and the teenage years. Parents and adults with teenagers often reap the results of how they tackled moral development in the early years. Children brought up in the early years to explore the following areas are not so likely to become delinquent teenagers:

* intention when things go wrong;
* empathising with how it feels to someone else when you do something that makes things go wrong;
* seeing the consequences of your actions;
* understanding cause-and-effect relationships of events and actions;
* how systems develop that are just and fair and that can be enforced – this means discussing rules, whether or not there is any flexibility in the rules;
* how to make sure those in authority are just and fair in the spirit in which they operate the system of justice.

Young children are dependent on parents, carers, teachers, friends of the family and older children to be fair in the way they are dealt with.

Adolescents and adults participate in the whole social justice system in their society and how it relates to their culture, for example issues such as the importance of policing by consent.

Judge Tumin (*Sunday Times* Lecture Series, 1994) said that one of the features of young offenders in his then role as Chief Inspector of Prisons was that they had little understanding of the difference between formal and informal situations and formal and informal behaviour. They tended to tell him personal details when he was a complete stranger to them, when in fact he was not a friend to be confided in. Roberts (2002) reports the importance of children learning to recognise the difference between informal behaviour at home and going out, and more formal behaviour in their family lives.

When she was three years of age, **HANNAH**'s mother explained that the family was going to meet someone from daddy's work, and it would be important to be on best behaviour. Hannah's response was 'no one say bloody'.

Adults who focus on positive role modelling, set clear boundaries, engage in positive negotiation and conflict resolution with plenty of discussion, demonstrating listening, talking and warm concern are more likely to encourage moral and social behaviour in young children, but also with a forward influence into adolescence and adulthood.

Knowing who you are and how you want to be

From an early age, children begin to tease out that what is appropriate behaviour in one cultural setting is not in another. For some children, the difference between school culture and home culture is slight; for others it is huge. This is important because the 'fitting in' is part of social and moral development.

It partly involves being able to be sensitive to those you are with, but it also involves remaining who you are in different situations. Being swayed away from what you normally do shows a weak sense of self-embodiment. Nikolai is being helped to develop a strong sense of who he wants to be.

> Six-year-old **NIKOLAI**'s mother thanked him for thinking of her by offering her one of his sweets. She praised his kindness but did not take one, thereby encouraging him to take such a risk again!

The damage done through herding children in large groups

Some adults demand too much from young children in this respect, for example sitting for long periods in school assembly at three and four years of age. It is inappropriate, and likely in the long run to put children off of trying to fit in with the system, and so ironically to damage their moral development. Young children are often accused of naughtiness during assemblies. In this case naughtiness is simply not doing what an adult wants. Young children are unlikely to be clear about the difference between naughtiness that inconveniences the system and the naughtiness of hitting someone else or stealing. For the young child in assembly, naughtiness becomes what adults do not like. The crucial dialogue, central to moral development and good behaviour long term, is missing. Without adult help, children cannot sort out the interplay between intention, motive, outcome and consequence.

When adults and atmospheres in settings are insensitive to children, children are insensitive to others

If the system is utterly insensitive to the child, we cannot expect the child to be sensitive to the system. The system is not, in this case, making appropriate demands on the child. It is also important to bear in mind that a child who can ask questions about 'why must we sit so long, it is boring' is actually thinking about the social conventions of life (in this case the inappropriateness of putting nursery Reception children into assembly).

In the days of Nazi Germany, or during Apartheid in South Africa, it took great courage to question the social conventions of these regimes. The 'fitting in' aspect of moral development must be seen side by side with the development of the child's conscience. It was the voices of individual conscience that led to the abolition of slavery and Apartheid, not the voices of those who 'fitted in'. The four-year-old who questions being made to sit still for long periods of time, such as in assembly, does not yet realise the enormity of the challenge that he or she is making, but that does not mean the child is wrong to challenge what many early childhood educators regard as a form of child abuse. There needs to be a balance between encouraging children to question, explore and develop a conscience over and above conforming to the socio-cultural conventions in which they live. It is important that adults do not let young children down by ignoring the questions they ask about these things, which help them to think about what is socially appropriate and morally right.

Three-year-old **AMANDIP** is beginning to use English in school. He is enjoying the fact that he can express himself in Punjabi and English. He chatters throughout group time and requests songs and sings them solo, because he cannot wait for the group. He wants to answer all the questions the teacher puts to the group of children. He is irrepressible. His teacher does not stop him; she encourages him, bringing in other children's contributions around his. She recognises his 'explosion' in English, but she does gently insist that the group finishes one song before he suggests another.

Research (Kitzinger, 1997: 16) indicates that, in a group, most people become passive and the 'bystander effect' operates, so that if, for example, someone is attacked in front of the group, often no one does anything. It takes leadership to step out of being in a group and to call the police. This has serious implications for young children.

If children are herded about in large groups for large parts of their day (as they often are in large Reception classes), the 'bystander effect' is encouraged and moral behaviour is discouraged. Children in smaller, intimate, quality early years settings are more likely to respond to situations as individuals and to learn to empathise and show care.

Helping social, emotional, spiritual and moral development

* Social, emotional, spiritual and moral development is helped when children are treated sensitively by adults.
* It is helped when there is plenty of discussion and negotiation in the family and early years settings.
* Children need to feel closeness, trust and understanding with adults who explain things to them, and help them to express their thoughts and feelings about issues and events.
* Children help each other through the quarrels they have and the negotiating and discussing they do.
* Free-flow play (Bruce, 1991) encourages children to see things from other people's points of view as they move in to and out of different roles and imaginary situations.
* Giving rewards for good behaviour undermines long-term moral and social development (Kohn, 1993).

How adults can help social, emotional, spiritual and moral development in the young child

Parents and practitioners working together in partnership

In the children's centre, the practitioner was doing a project on 'flowers'. She had an interest table full of them, with some that children could take apart and look at under magnifying glasses. Three-year-old **MELISSA** enjoyed putting things inside others (a topological, spatial schema in Piaget's theory). She homed in on this interest table, and began putting flowers into vases with gusto. At home time the early years worker explained this interest to her mother and asked her if she would like to take the pot of flowers home to follow up the school work. Melissa's mother had problems in getting her to come to the table at mealtimes because she always wanted to bring her toys with her. She found that by asking Melissa to put some flowers (even weeds from the garden) in a vase on the table she could overcome this problem. Delighted, she told the practitioner about this in school next day. This marked a turning point for Melissa, who began to help her mother prepare the table for meals at home and then sat down readily.

The difference between social and moral rules

Turiel and Weston (1983) demonstrated that by the age of five years, children can distinguish between different types of rules. Moral rules (it is wrong to hit) were regarded as unchangeable. Social rules (you must tidy the room before going out) could be changed. The EPPE study (2003) suggests that two-year-olds in quality group day care are more socially developed later in the primary school. This does not mean that they are more morally and spiritually developed.

The importance of play with other children

Group situations with peers, more and less advanced and at the same stage, are important during early childhood. Group play involves children in giving up their immediate wishes in order that the play can continue successfully. Vygotsky (1978) sees this as an important attribute.

A shoe shop had been set up in the classroom. The family of four-year-old **NEELAN** owns a shop. She wanted the early years worker to pretend to be the shopkeeper, who quickly assumed that role. She took younger children, three-year-olds **SHAZIA** and **TOTO**, as customers. Certainly she dominated the play, but she was inducting them into what imaginative play is about. They willingly stayed, but could have left at any time. Toto and Shazia needed Neelan to show them how to play 'pretend games', how to take roles and become other people, how to decentre and see other viewpoints.

ANNA MARIA is another typical three-year-old. The practitioner was working with a group of children on the large wooden blocks. They (two girls and two boys) were sitting on them as a table and chairs. Four-year-old **TRACY** brought a small wooden block and said, 'Would you like a tin of beans?' and laughed. The teacher said, 'I'd love some – but I need to open the tin.' She pretended to do this to a rapt audience. Then she asked for a saucepan in which to heat the beans. **SADE** found a flatter cylinder (a thoroughly appropriate representation of a saucepan). The teacher pretended to pour in the beans and stir. Then she asked for some plates. The children found more blocks and the teacher made toast using rectangular shapes. At this point Anna Maria came in and watched the activity. She came up to the teacher and said triumphantly, 'You're only pretending, you know.' She did not want to join in; she only wanted to watch the game.

Young children need to see high-level imaginative play before being helped into it. This has implications for later work in school. Getting on the inside of roles and themes in imaginative play requires the child to go beyond 'self' and to 'become' other people in other situations in a meaningful context. Becoming someone else, acting out a role and a theme, requires considerable tuning in to self and others, reading situations, and coordinating different points of view and feelings. The spontaneous scripts that develop during imaginative play are the stuff of later story writing. This form of play encourages the embryonic sense of audience that will flower later on.

Seven-year-old **HANNAH**, three-year-old **KIT**, and five-year-olds **MATTHEW** and **WILLIAM** decide to play King Arthur. Only Hannah and William know the story and the game quickly disintegrates. All the children know the story of Robin Hood.

Hannah suggests that they play this instead and she coordinates the story. There is a lot of discussion: 'You say "I am hurt" and I say "Get up"', and so on. The script is agreed and carried out in action. All dress up in clothes from the dressing-up box, with swords. Kit (the youngest) follows. He makes mistakes, goes to the wrong place, kills the 'wrong' person and the other children (mainly Hannah) alert him to what is needed. Interestingly, in games of mixed ages or large groups of children, there often seems to be a great deal of rushing about and follow-my-leader activity. Younger children need the stimulation and leadership of more advanced children. Older children need to lead and organise complicated games, with younger children as willing participants.

Hannah, if the game is to succeed, needs to help Kit by trying to see his difficulties. She needs to keep William and Matthew happy about Kit's 'errors', and to negotiate, smooth situations over and make acceptable suggestions. Maid Marian, she points out, when Matthew makes a bid to become leader of the game, is as good at shooting arrows as Robin Hood. Matthew is Robin Hood. He insists that he is a better archer. William supports Hannah. 'It's in the book,' he declares. Hannah gets round this by suggesting that they all surround the Sheriff of Nottingham (a bush in the garden), but do not kill him. Group play, like partnership play, is important in helping children to develop the ability to empathise and develop theory of mind. In these ways children begin to put themselves into other people's feelings and thoughts, while remaining themselves.

The long-term undermining impact of extrinsic reward

Extrinsic rewards for good behaviour are effective only in the short term, and according to Kohn (1993) may well inflict long-term damage to moral and social behaviour. He suggests that:

* rewards punish because they control us; feeling controlled by others damages autonomous learning (Principles 4 and 5);
* rewards damage a sense of collaboration and teamwork, or community; they are divisive because they set children against each other as rivals;
* rewards mask problems and ignore reasons why children or adults behave as they do;
* rewards discourage risk taking because they assume children are naturally lazy rather than naturally adventurous and creative;
* rewards damage genuine interest by implying that it is not worth being good for its own sake; rewards undermine intrinsic motivation.

Being controlled by extrinsic rewards does not lead to fulfilment. Being controlled by the rewards that others in positions of power give for hard work is not empowering. It creates dependency on and the need to please those who hold power. It means competing with peers in order to gain prizes, so that ruthlessness towards others easily develops. It is sometimes argued that we need to reward ourselves with treats when a task is completed in order to motivate ourselves. But completion of the task is the reward. Nelson Mandela did not develop the groundbreaking Council of Reconciliation because he was told he would be rewarded with a prize if he did so. He did not give himself a prize either. He did the work because he believed it is better to encourage those who have committed atrocities to reflect on what they have done and to truly see the consequences of their actions, and for those who have suffered to see that this, punishment as an attempt to reform wrongdoers, is a better way forward than using punishment as revenge. The Nobel Prize for Peace that was awarded to Mandela was entirely different from a reward used to goad someone into a required action. This was an acknowledgement of the deep contribution his influence has had in developing peace-making progress that is ethically framed.

Perhaps the last word should go to six-year-old Maisie. The head teacher came into the classroom and said to a group of children engaged in a mathematical calculation, 'If you can give the right answer, I will give you a star.' Maisie said, 'I will give you the answer, but I don't need the star.' The reward, as Maisie knows, is getting the right answer. That is satisfying, inwardly. Maisie is intrinsically motivated. She works hard for her own feeling of fulfilment. She is not extrinsically motivated, always doing things to please others or to have proof of her success in a reward form. She has no need for a star chart for herself, or for her class. It is concerning that extrinsic motivation seems to be widespread in its application in current practice. It prevents the development of intrinsic motivation where it is not in place, and it undermines it where it exists.

Summary – learning how you and others feel and think

Even babies and toddlers recognise and imitate feelings from other people. Real empathy and being able to put yourself in someone else's shoes comes from toddler times onwards, so that children:

* develop a conscience (moral values that are not just about obeying what adults and authority figures say is right and good);
* learn how to make and change rules (laws) and to see why they are needed;
* behave thoughtfully, influenced by their inner values more than by external rewards.

Knowing right from wrong means:

* judging someone's intention;
* recognising how much children know and understand;
* seeing the consequences of actions and words.

Moral development is helped when children's self-esteem is not undermined by being told they are naughty or bad children. Rejecting what they have done, but valuing, respecting and loving them unconditionally helps children to discuss the results of their actions, and how this makes other people feel (Dunn, 1988).

Moral development is concerned with

* moral values;
* moral behaviour.

Children who are supported and helped to reflect on their feelings, ideas and relationships develop a strong sense of embodied self, and well-being. This developing self-awareness takes place as they relate to others, especially those with whom they develop close and intimate relationships. Being helped to read and tune in to the feelings and thoughts of others leads to empathy and theory of mind, and the understanding that others feel and think differently because they are individuals who are unique.

The spiritual development of children is about the way they relate to self, others and the universe.

9

People who matter to children

Introduction

This chapter looks at people who matter to young children. Urie Bronfenbrenner developed what is now known as a bio-ecological systems theory (Ryan, 2010), which proposes that a child's development occurs within a system of relationships. This involves the biological development of the child, the family environment and the societal landscape.

Biology fuels development in this theory, and so the child's biological development is crucial. At different points of biological development a child will respond differently, for example, to grandmother's death, as a toddler or as a four-year-old, or seven-year-old. This is called the chronosystem. The death is an event external to the child, but the point of development of the child will influence how the child responds to the death. So will other factors, such as the microsystem of the family, school or early childhood setting and the neighbourhood community. There will be what Bronfenbrenner calls bidirectional influences. Children are both influenced, for example, by their parents, but they also influence them, bringing ideas and thoughts from the school and community they spend time with. The way that the family, carers and teacher/early childhood practitioner link with each other is part of the mesosystem. The circle of people widens out to include society as a whole, including the professional workers in statutory and voluntary agencies with whom the family/carer has contact. This is part of the exosystem.

The different parts of the system influence and impact on each other; and the macrosystem shows the way in which values, custom and laws do so.

The way that children interact with each other and form relationships is explored first in this chapter. Children relating to other children is a theme that pervades this book. It is at the heart of the Froebelian approach to education.

Other children

In Chapter 8, the importance of the relationships children develop with brothers, sisters and close friends was emphasised.

Groups

Zick Rubin (1983) suggests that there are four ways in which children need to develop skills in getting on with other children. These are:

1. to be able to gain entry into a group;
2. to be approving and supportive of one's peers;
3. to manage conflicts appropriately;
4. to exercise sensitivity and tact.

The examples that follow show Rubin's (1983) four strategies in action.

In a nursery school, a group of children were playing pirates. The pirate ship was a scrambling net on a prism-shaped climbing frame. The game involved climbing the 'rigging' and, when another ship was spotted from afar, rushing out and capturing treasure from it, and returning with the booty. The enemy ship would be an agreed place where there was a pile of leaves. The leaves were then brought back as booty.

The children were predominantly four years of age. Four-year-old JAMES was the pirate leader. Three-year-old ALICE wanted to join in. She watched from a distance, walking round the edge of the playground.

She approached and stood hopefully at the foot of the climbing frame/pirate ship. She was ignored. She began to climb the net with the others, smiling at her success. As James shouted, 'Ahoy there – a ship. Let's go!' and scrambled down, hotly pursued by the others shouting 'Let's go!', she imitated them. She had been watching for long enough to know that she needed to pick up leaves from the pile. She had successfully joined the game.

William Corsaro's work (1979) suggests that Alice's tactics were typical of successful 'access strategies' for entering into the game. She encircled the game, made careful 'verbal overtures', joining in with the other children's 'Let's go!', did similar things to them and so was not rejected.

Four-year-old Mathilde wanted to join a group of children in the home corner. She tried to walk in through the door, saying, 'Can I play?' 'No,' shouted the other children in chorus, and shut the door on her. She had not had the opportunity to encircle, and her opening conversation invited rejection.

Corsaro's (1979) work suggests that children need to use 'similar behaviour' in order to be accepted. Mathilde could not see what was behind the door, so she was not in a position to engage in similar behaviour in her actions, or to back this up with remarks such as, 'We're moving the furniture, aren't we?' William Corsaro calls this kind of remark 'reference to affiliation'.

In Chapter 8 there are many examples that are relevant to the significant other children in any child's life. Group play offers children the opportunity to see things from other people's points of view. It also offers the child possibilities to experiment with relating to others in a safe way. In Chapter 6 further examples of group play have been given. Adults often find large groups difficult to justify as educationally worthwhile. Some children tend to be involved in this sort of activity almost to the exclusion of any other if given the choice. In the examples in this chapter, and in other chapters of this book, it emerges that group play is an important but undervalued aspect of what early childhood practice can offer. Adults need to develop skills in encouraging and promoting this.

> Four-year-old **GAVIN** started to put large wooden bricks round the edge of the room. Other children copied. Adults intervened when quarrels broke out, or if other equipment that children were using needed to be moved. Soon there was an enclosure of bricks round the whole room. Children began to move around them as if they were stepping stones. About 15 children had become involved in this joint activity. Adults had taken a supportive role, letting children watch until they were 'ready' to join in, altering the physical environment in discussion with the children.

Group times, when children come together for stories, music, singing, dancing or physical education, are naturally more adult-led than child-initiated. These can be difficult times for a considerable proportion of children, particularly in the earliest years. So far as this chapter is concerned, it is sufficient to say that sitting with a friend often helps children to settle in to a group time most easily. The comfort of sitting with a friend is a powerful support.

Partnerships

> **LINDSEY** and **BARBARA**, two three-year-olds, are playing horses together. Lindsey puts a long belt around Barbara's waist and 'leads' her. She rehearses what she is going to say so that Barbara is in on the script.
>
> 'I say, "Whoa there!" don't I, and you go, "Neigh", don't you, and then I pat you and I give you some hay, don't I, and you bend down like this, and you eat it, don't you?' Then they act out the scene. This helps the children to plan their story in advance, to be clear about the theme and their roles in it.

It is interesting to note that at this time, both Lindsey and Barbara showed interest in things that could be made to encircle. The belt surrounds Barbara's waist. Early friendships are said to be fleeting; one possibility is that they may be based on shared interests and that, when these change, the friendship loses its base. After all, the basis of any friendship lies in having shared interests.

It is also interesting that this play scenario was based on a shared experience. The group had been taken to see the police stables, and had been shown the harnesses. The play centred primarily around harnessing and unharnessing a horse. Shared interests and experiences are fundamental aspects of early partnerships.

Six-year-olds Dominic and Michael had both seen a fight on the television. They were acting out a shared secondary experience with a lot of 'stop–go' in this game: careful play punching, holding at gun point, kicking to the ground. No one gets hurt. This is the sort of play that adults find difficult to allow (Holland, 2003). This kind of play, when indulged in by girls, tends to be firmly squashed. In fact, the skill that lies in not hurting each other, the refinement and variety of movement, the planning together, rehearsing and carrying out of the plan, is not unlike the processes of draft, revise, redraft, refine, which are involved in story writing. It is important to recognise the sophistication that may have developed. The kind of play that Michael and Dominic were involved in was not simply rumbustious. It was helping the children to develop on a variety of levels.

There is a range of people who are significant in one way or another to the development of a young child. In particular, family, professional workers and other children whom the child meets regularly all become important for that child in a direct way. In this chapter, the impact of the family, professional workers and other children is discussed in turn, with particular reference to the role of the early childhood practitioner.

Family and carers

Gillian Pugh and Erica De'Ath (1984: 169) state that:

> The great majority of parents are concerned to do their best for their children, even if they are not always sure what this might be.

More recent research suggests that parents/carers are not clear what quality provision involves (Goouch and Lambirth, 2007; Owen, 2009), and that they rely on the recommendation of friends or the view of official experts in making choices (Ofsted).

Every family is different, and has different needs. The key to partnership with parents lies in having a network of strategies that can be employed so that different approaches are used with different families, approaches that support and build on the families rather than undermining what the parents/carers do. Some families do not wish to or cannot come into school often. With the increased number of divorced parents, there are often issues of whether parents will attend school together, and both parents wanting to be informed about their child's progress. Some families enjoy being in school or an early years setting, but in the parents' room. Others prefer to be visited at home. All parents need to feel they belong in the setting, and this is particularly important for parents of minority groups, such as same-sex parents, or parents with disabilities. For example, parents with a hearing impairment might need a British Sign Language interpreter. Others want workshops, meetings, films, talks in the evenings or at weekends, after school, often provided that there is a crèche. Others will make equipment, raise funds, come to social functions but do not want further contact. Some parents actively seek help in child rearing and in the education of their children, others do not.

The early years worker's role is to build a partnership with every parent. Clearly, it is easier to do this with some parents than with others. Situations involving suspected child abuse, whether physical, mental or sexual, are the most difficult and, where this exists, the staff need to work with other professionals as much as with the parents.

However, the tendency of professionals to undermine any parent's self-confidence with their 'expertise', and the isolation felt by many bringing up young children, contribute to the difficulties experienced by many parents/carers.

Most parents are not interested in children in general. Their main concern is with their own child and the child's friends. They are not teachers, nor do they wish to be. Practitioners and parents do not bring the same qualities to the partnership. Their roles are complementary, and should not be seen as threatening to each other.

The parent/carer is highly emotionally linked to the child, and prepared to go to 'unreasonable lengths' for the child, as shown by Elizabeth Newson's study (1972; quoted in Kellmer Pringle, 1980: 37).

Parents want their children to be happy in school or in any kind of early childhood group care setting, or with a childminder in a home learning environment. So do early childhood practitioners. The key person is a crucial role, and has become increasingly embedded in practice in the UK.

The key person

Peter Elfer (Elfer, Goldschmied and Selleck, 2003) is a leading expert on the role of the key person, and has worked with Julian Grenier and Julia Manning-Morton, supporting practitioners in leadership positions. The key person role has arisen out of attachment theory, pioneered by John Bowlby. This means that young children experience a 'close continuous relationship with a small number of main carers, normally parents and close family members' (Elfer and Grenier, 2010). This is not the same as saying that only the mother can care for the child in this way. There has been a misinterpretation of John Bowlby's work in this respect. The important thing is that attachments are crucial to the emotional and social health of very young children. Different cultures approach attachment in very different ways. This is the case whether children are in the family most of the time, with a childminder in a home learning environment, or in group care.

Bronfenbrenner's mesosystem is useful here. The way that a child placed in day care or with a childminder relates to their key person will be of central importance; so too is the relationship between the parents and the key person. When these significant people for the child work well together, then the experience in a day care or childminding context is likely to be a positive one for the child, family and the practitioner. The same is true for parents bringing up their child with one parent staying at home, or with both parents working part-time.

Elfer and Grenier (2010: 150) point out the complexity, both emotionally and at an organisational level, of forming close personal relationships with children within the professional context. There is a need for openness and accountability.

Figure 9.1: Father collects his child – the key person is involved in this transitional moment.

Staff need to have general responsibility for children and to work as a team, and they emphasise that moving staff to have sufficient cover across the setting needs some thought. Children will have preferences and staff may need support in this. Parents will be both pleased and anxious as their child becomes close to their key person. Staff will need to reassure parents that they are not taking the place of the parent.

The triangle of child, parent and key person is a complex set of relationships, but it is an important one.

Transitions

Educators who look below the surface of what parents/carers are saying can find a shared basis for work on which trust can be built. Parents want their children to be successful at reading, writing and mathematics, and to be well behaved and popular. So do staff. The aims of parents and teachers in fact coincide in important areas. But teachers need to share what they know about child development and curriculum provision, rather than guard their knowledge. When parents/carers and practitioners build their observations of children together, and use them to inform the next steps in planning for the child's learning, the impact is deep.

The Froebel Nursery Research Project emphasised parent/staff partnership (Athey, 1990) and found that different parents liked to work with staff in different ways, with different parenting styles. It was important therefore that the teacher tuned in to the particular needs of individual families. There is no one way to work with parents.

The following examples show how staff can work with a wide variety of parents, as described below.

* Parents recognising or trying to extend the learning of their child.
* Parents who are eager to work with staff in early childhood settings in ways that do not fit in with the teacher's methods.
* Parents bodily in the early childhood setting, but not active in the classroom.
* Parents whose main contact with the setting is bringing and fetching children, and perhaps attending parents' evenings.
* Parents who do not bring children to the early childhood setting, or seek contact with the staff.

Figure 9.2: The key person is settling the little girl. She stays near her, but does not invade her space while she wants to experience things on her own. But the key person is there if she is needed. Settling children in with a good transition is one of the most important things early years practitioners do.

Parents recognising or trying to extend the learning of the child

Three-year-old **SHANAZ**'s father was a bus driver. He wanted to be with his children as much as possible, and managed to arrange his shift work accordingly. He brought Shanaz to the early childhood setting whenever he could and normally stayed for half an hour. (He brought his younger child, a toddler, with him, too.) He wanted to know what was the purpose of each activity. He took great pleasure in watching Shanaz in the nursery once he realised that water play and other messy activities could be used to teach her mathematical language (for example, 'out of the water', 'in the water', 'high', 'low', 'long way', and so on). He used these terms with relish as she played. He was 'teaching' his daughter mathematics. His enthusiasm was invigorating for the staff, who found him a positive adult to welcome in to the school. His basic trust of the teachers' knowledge made it easier for the school staff to work with him.

Parents who are eager to work with practitioners in ways that do not fit in with the practitioners' methods

It is not for practitioners to tell families how to bring up their children, nor to insist that learning must be approached in one way. Just as staff need to establish a child's intentions and build on them in worthwhile ways, so they need to find out what parents think quality learning is, before they can begin a successful partnership with parents/carers.

All too often the parents/carers are asked to listen to the staff's view, but not the reverse. Parents/carers need to know what staff are trying to do, but staff need to know what parents/carers consider to be important. This is the basis of mutual respect – that is, respect for each other's expertise, respect for each other's commitment to a particular child, respect for the different skills and strengths each brings to a complementary partnership. Two examples follow that show how the practitioner can use his or her skills to encourage appropriate parental involvement.

Five-year-old **BETTY**'s mother liked to work in the early childhood setting. She was eager to 'teach' an activity. The practitioner suggested that she helped the children to make dough and use it. She wanted Betty's mother to see her do this activity with the children before she had a group on her own. Betty's mother could not resist joining in while the practitioner worked with the group. The practitioner asked an open-ended question: 'I wonder what we do first?' Betty's mother instantly swooped in: 'We need a bowl, spoon and flour.' She began transmitting the knowledge. This was how she saw the role of the 'teacher', not asking obtuse questions that did not get to the point. The practitioner suggested that Betty's mother should check all the time what children had learned by asking them questions about what they were doing. Betty's mother accepted this and acted on it, as it was part of her view of learning – teach the knowledge, then test the knowledge. Over a period of a year Betty's mother and the practitioner began to discuss the importance of getting children to anticipate what will happen, to plan what will happen, to organise equipment they will need. Initially, the practitioner built on the parent's view of a teacher's role, and so did not undermine her confidence and did not reject her views.

Some parents experience difficulty in leaving their child in school. They are sometimes unfairly referred to as clinging or over-protective. They are often parents who enjoy a very close relationship with their children, and are very sensitive to their child's feelings and deeply concerned about their child's education.

When five-year-old **STEPHANIE** made a preliminary visit to the Reception class, prior to beginning school, her mother instantly settled down to work with her and the group of children at the construction toy table. She talked to each child about what he or she was doing, and skilfully involved Stephanie in contributing and in talking to the child next to her; so far, so good. When Stephanie began to attend regularly at school, her mother wanted to stay until she was 'settled'. The teacher suggested, on the second day, that her mother should take a short coffee break in the staff room. Stephanie cried. Mother would not leave her.

Next day, Stephanie began to cling to her mother all the time, anticipating that she would try to have coffee. Mother reassured her, insisting that she would not leave her at all. Stephanie wanted to keep her mother very close to her, and stopped attempting to relate to the other children. By the end of the week, the pattern was set. Stephanie would not become involved in activities. Neither could her mother become involved, because Stephanie thwarted any attempt she made to work with groups of children. Stephanie's mother was upset. She felt that she had done all the 'right things', and yet her child would not let her go at all. Her 'good' mothering was being punished instead of rewarded. She needed the teacher as someone to help her who was not involved in this 'eyeball-to-eyeball' situation.

The teacher could not discuss anything with the mother since Stephanie clung to her, so she asked her to phone from home. The teacher then discussed strategies, telling her that this was a not uncommon experience for very good, sensitive, devoted parents. Of course, Stephanie did not want such a treasured person to leave. She suggested that Stephanie's mother and school take a united approach, and insist that she left for 15 minutes immediately on school arrival, warning Stephanie that this would happen. In this way, Stephanie did not have the worry of anticipating her mother's going until coffee time. They would gradually increase the time out, agreeing its length in discussion together. Once Stephanie was settled, her mother would be able to come into school and work with the children, say once a week, since she wanted to be involved in the classroom. At this stage, it would be too complicated for Stephanie to grasp that pattern. They needed to wait until she was established. In this way, the teacher reassured the mother that she could be trusted with her child, and would be sensitive towards her. She made it clear that she thought highly of her parenting, understood her child's behaviour and wanted to welcome her to the classroom in principle, but the timing of this had to revolve around what would be appropriate for Stephanie. Stephanie's mother relaxed. So did Stephanie, who settled in to school happily during that term. The next term, her mother came regularly to school to help with cooking, reading, model making, and so on.

Parents bodily in the early childhood setting, but not actively participating

Some parents, if encouraged, will often linger after having brought their child to the setting, but will resist greater involvement. The early childhood practitioner needs to develop strategies for encouraging the parents' interest in their children into active expression.

Three-year-old **KHALIQ**'s mother regularly brought him to the early years setting, and went immediately to the book corner, where she was friendly, but did not seek contact with the practitioner while her child settled in to the group. Khaliq's mother was in the setting regularly, but as yet there was no partnership with the practitioner. Each week there was cookery, and the practitioner asked her if she would make chapattis with the children. She said her English was not good enough, but the teacher encouraged her to speak in Urdu. She enjoyed the cookery session, and stayed on for the end-of-the-morning singing, sitting with the practitioner and children. She liked the songs, which included 'Humpty Dumpty'. The practitioner explained that the song was to help the children use mathematical language ('up' and 'down'), and that tomorrow she would do 'The Grand Old Duke of York'. She invited the mother to join the session. Mother was delighted, and was heard saying 'up' and 'down' to Khaliq as they went out. The next step was to encourage the mother to watch her child with the practitioner. Khaliq was observed putting a pile of bricks into the classroom 'telephone kiosk' one by one, and then, once a pile had formed, picking each one up and throwing it into a large cardboard box outside the kiosk. He did this for some time. He was transporting, and placing objects in containers. The member of staff asked if he did anything like this at home. He had put a pile of dried chick-peas into a saucepan from a colander, but his mother could not explain this in English. She demonstrated with equipment in the home corner, and the following day brought in chick-peas and demonstrated again. Meanwhile, the staff had organised a paint-mixing activity with Khaliq in mind. This involved putting powder paint into pots and adding water. Khaliq did this for half an hour. His mother was beginning to see how reporting his home activities to the practitioner was important, as the staff used this information in their lesson planning. She began to see that activities were planned, and that mess was necessary and could lead to science. The 'mixtures' were an early chemistry lesson, the teacher explained. So was the cookery lesson, making chapattis. These were both examples of changing a substance: from powder (paint) to sludgy liquid (paint and water) and from powdery flour to a solid chapatti. This activity is a precursor to understanding chemical equations. Khaliq's mother could see that the staff wanted him to learn mathematics (up and down songs). She gradually became more relaxed about messy activities because she could see that they led on to science and maths.

Staff need to share the importance of these different areas of learning with parents. Valuing messy home activities (cookery), and giving them high status in school, is one starting point. Khaliq's mother also liked gardening, and grew vegetables in school, as she lived in a flat with no garden.

Outdoor activities were then given high value. This is another area that is often not understood to be important by parents/carers. Studying worms, snails, slugs and the different properties of soils (clay, sand and gravel) is messy, but leads to natural science. By beginning with what the parent valued, cooking and gardening, the practitioner was able to share the importance of messy and outdoor activities with this parent, over a period of time. Khaliq's mother also began, very gradually, to see the need to observe the child before planning lessons, so that the lesson was effective and appropriate, and to see that her observations mattered as well as the teacher's. She became active in the classroom, cooking, gardening, helping with paintings and so on, using her strengths. She was a home garment maker, and a sewing machine was set up for her in the classroom where she made clothes for the dressing-up corner, or for her child, out of a big box of materials that was always available; and she let the children have turns, too.

She did not see herself as a teacher. Her presence enriched the activities, introduced Urdu alongside English, and helped the staff through her developing skill in observing her own child. Her interest was in her child. In doing the activities she enjoyed, in which the children participated, she enhanced rather than threatened the teacher's role.

Khaliq's father visited the school to 'inspect it' when Khaliq first came. The practitioner talked about his learning, mainly the beginning of the three Rs. Khaliq's father came when dolls' wash day was in progress. He was about to leave this 'women's activity' and take his son to something else. The practitioner explained to him that this was a mathematics lesson. She told him that she and his wife had noted Khaliq transporting objects and putting them into containers. This washing activity had been designed to help Khaliq to do both. It helped his ability to make a series (largest, smallest clothes to peg out); it helped him to classify (soapy water, rinsing water, and so on). She explained that Khaliq needed to both seriate and classify in order to be ready for number work later on. She demonstrated this difficult theory in a practical context. Father and son stayed at the activity. Khaliq's father did not visit again, but gave his approval for his wife to continue bringing Khaliq.

The developing partnership in Khaliq's family took a year to become established, and a further year to flourish. Most teachers work with a group of children for only one year and so the importance of working with colleagues as a team, and of a whole-school policy in relation to work with parents, requires emphasis. The importance of five terms in the nursery where the partnership pattern is established also requires consideration.

This example also demonstrates the indirect approach to structuring learning in the interactionist style. One of the central aims of this approach is to respect and include the parent/carer's view

Parents whose main contact with the school is bringing and fetching children, and attending parents' evening

Five-year-old **KIM**'s mother brought and fetched her each day; she would have a quick chat with the teacher, but had shown no sign of wishing to become involved in the classroom. She was anxious for Kim to learn to read and write. As is quite common, she saw teaching Kim to do this as the main function of school. She had taught Kim to write her name before she came to school.

There was a problem here in that the mother was also encouraging Kim to copy words. This differed from the school's approach, which advocated children constructing their own letters when writing and where children are introduced to conventional spelling as involving problem solving. Here was a clash between home and school. Kim's mother was not going to be convinced that the way she herself learned to write 'was wrong', because she successfully learned to write that way. The teacher organised an exhibition of written work from Reception to top infants, asking her colleagues to help her. As parents brought their children in or collected them, she referred to this. She showed Kim's mother what the school did. Kim's mother was reassured to see the high standard of spelling and large amounts of creative writing many children achieved later in the school. She was interested to see writing including stories and poems, describing outings or events, annotating of models they had made or writing up experiments they had performed. In this way, Kim's mother was introduced to different modes of writing. Her concept of 'writing' broadened, but the teacher did not undermine her. She congratulated the mother on teaching Kim the alphabet and especially on starting with the letters of her name. She was pleased that she had taught Kim to be enthusiastic about writing and to feel that she could write. She asked her to write down stories Kim wanted to tell, so that she (as teacher) could make them into a book for Kim. As Kim was not used to 'inventing' spelling with her mother, the teacher worked on this aspect with her in school. In this way, she protected the child/parent relationship from possible failure during what might have been a difficult transition.

Once Kim became confident in her own ability to 'have a go' at spelling, she began spontaneously to do this with her mother. Her mother did not automatically 'correct' the spelling. She left it unless it was one of the spellings she and the teacher had decided to work on (for example 'wood' for 'would'). The teacher said, when Kim's mother met her from school that she wanted to work on the 'would' family of words, since Kim consistently spelled this sound 'oo'.

Home and school were working together successfully. Kim's mother had not been asked to abandon her view of how children learn to write. She had broadened it, which had been an exciting rather than an undermining experience. In this partnership, it was the ten minutes before and after school that were of critical importance. Kim's mother also attended any evening 'talks' to parents about different aspects of the curriculum.

Parents who do not bring children to school, or seek contact with school

When this unusual situation arises, it is important for the practitioners working with the family to attempt to make contact with the parents/carers, in a sensitive way. The challenge is how. Three-year-old Jerome's parents did not attempt any contact with the school until the teacher sought it. Indeed, they seemed quite apathetic, and involvement with them required intermediary help from the health visitor. This example is discussed in full in the next section (on multi-agency work) because, as in many instances of complete lack of contact with parents, the support of other professional workers was necessary.

A network of strategies

Different families have different needs. Having a variety of approaches helps the parent/carer/staff partnership to develop with success, which means that significant people in the child's life are working together for the child.

In the next section, which looks at the way professionals in statutory and voluntary agencies work with parents, the need for early childhood practitioners to work with a variety of adults as well as parents is emphasised. Being child-centred is too narrow an approach. It is more appropriate to consider the child-in-context, and that includes the different skills and strengths that different professionals and voluntary agencies have to offer in strengthening the child, as a member of a family. The developments of *Every Child Matters* from 2004 give five strands that will impact on every area of early childhood practice. These have arisen from consultation with children, young people and families. They are:

1. being healthy;
2. staying safe;
3. enjoying and achieving;
4. making a positive contribution;
5. economic well-being.

Figure 9.3: The adult is playing with the child in the sandpit. This helps the child to make the transition of their mother leaving them. The child is supported through this with interesting conversation and being involved in something they find interesting.

Multi-agency work

In the early stages of the child's life, the GP and health visitor are likely to be key professionals. Health visitors can act as catalysts for family development in coordination with other professionals.

JANE

One-year-old Jane's family disliked professional workers as they had had a number of unfortunate experiences over the years. The health visitor found it difficult to gain entrance to their flat, and yet she and the GP were concerned about Jane's physical growth and weight. She was small for her age, and not eating well. She was too young to attend a playgroup, and there was no parent/toddler group within easy walking distance.

Another of the health visitor's clients had been a nursery teacher until she gave up work to have her child, now a one-year-old, and this mother ran a very small parent/toddler group that met three mornings a week. The health visitor put the two mothers in touch. Because the ex-nursery teacher was 'just another mother' with a one-year-old, she was able to work well with the family. Jane and her mother joined the group of four mothers and four children.

Relationships with the health visitor improved. She was seen as someone who could help, but not interfere. Visits to a specialist doctor were positive. The father attended the group when his shift work allowed. They all went to a swimming club together, and had joint outings and celebrated birthdays together, as well as undertaking joint jam making and bread making as part of the parent/toddler group activities. The health visitor was asked to provide information regularly. She organised visits from experts on preventive dentistry, family planning and nutrition, and gave information about different nursery provision in the area. At three years of age, Jane attended a larger playgroup so that her mother could work in the mornings. At four years, she attended the Reception class of the local school. The health visitor put the playgroup leader in touch with the parent/toddler group leader when a problem arose over Jane's eating. This was quickly resolved. In this example, the health visitor had coordinated and used the different local resources and called upon specialist medical advice in her attempt to help Jane's family. She was sufficiently skilled to use a volunteer worker's skills when her 'professionalism' was acting as a block in the early stages of her relationship with the family. She valued what other workers could offer at every stage. In Jane's case, it was the statutory services that 'led', with the health visitor as the key worker, coordinating GP, volunteer worker, playgroup and teacher, as well as specialist medical help.

In the following example, the health visitor again 'led'.

PETRA

Petra was born blind. She lived in an area where there was no special education support. Her parents were helped initially by the GP and health visitor, who put them in touch with an educational home visitor from a voluntary agency for the blind (Royal National Institute for the Blind). This professional worker helped the family through the first five years of Petra's life, and coordinated resources and professional help to such an extent that Petra was able to attend the local primary school. The role of this professional worker was also to offer emotional support to the family, and to act as a bridge between teachers in the school and the family when problems arose, which they did frequently.

There was a gap in statutory services for this family – no advice on how to stimulate and manage Petra in the first five years, and no school for visually impaired children at statutory school age. The LEA bought special school places from the neighbouring authority. The parents wanted Petra to attend school more locally and to have friends in the community if possible.

The educational home visitor gathered resources for the family with specialist equipment and advice on working with Petra in the earliest years. She supported them in the educational decisions they made and bridged the gap between home and school. She was a highly trained, paid worker, employed by a voluntary agency, who had more impact on this family's life in the first five years of Petra's life than any statutory worker because of her skill in coordinating the medical and educational resources available.

In the example of Jerome, which follows, the specialist nursery teacher was the key worker.

JEROME

Three-year-old Jerome's parents did not come to school. On his first day at school he was sent on the school bus alone under the care of the bus supervisor and driver. He was 'deaf', but his hearing aid was in his satchel. It would be easy for the teacher to draw the conclusion that here was an uncaring family, insensitive to their child's needs. The teacher in this special school used a home/school book with each family since children were spread over a large catchment area and were brought to school by bus. She immediately, on that first day, sent a book home in Jerome's satchel, asking if she could introduce herself to the parents, and wondering if they might like to visit the school.

The next day, the book had not been written in. The teacher could not phone the family as there was no phone, so she phoned the GP. He was wary of divulging any information at all, but grudgingly gave the name of the health visitor for the family. Contact with the health visitor revealed that both parents worked and were bewildered by their son Jerome, who had seemed to hear and had begun to talk at two years. He had recently been sent to Jamaica to stay with his grandmother for six months – and had stopped talking. On returning home he had been tested and found to have a hearing loss.

The health visitor agreed to find out if the family would like the teacher to visit. Two days later there was a note in the home book suggesting the teacher might like to call one day after school. The health visitor had found that the parents never looked in the satchel, so were unaware of the existence of the home book. The teacher set off on the school bus with

Jerome on the suggested day and, at the set-down point, found herself to her surprise at Jerome's childminder's flat. He would be picked up from there at 5.30 p.m. (It was now 4.30 p.m.) The childminder was obviously embarrassed about this, and so the teacher said that she had some shopping to do and would go straight to Jerome's flat later, which she did. When she met the parents at 6.00 p.m., a situation potentially damaging to the parent/teacher partnership had arisen. The parents were clearly embarrassed. To them 'after school' meant after work. They had not wanted the teacher to know that Jerome went to a childminder. They clearly thought that a teacher would disapprove of this.

If an atmosphere of trust and mutual respect were to develop, the teacher's training needed to be used. She had received considerable help in working with parents during her specialist training in working with hearing-impaired children. Over tea, she established an atmosphere whereby she made it clear that she was actively seeking the parents' views, and needed their help in order to do her job. The focus was on everyone working for Jerome. The parents admitted their anger that he had been sent to a special school and their perplexity that he had suddenly stopped talking. They talked about their dislike of the hearing aid, which labelled him. They did not want to come to school: they thought they would be upset to see other deaf children. Education to them meant learning to read, beginning with the alphabet, and they supposed that as Jerome was deaf there was no sense in trying to teach him. They just wanted him to be as happy as possible considering his disability. During the visit the teacher listened rather than talked. She also conveyed her delight in teaching Jerome; she wanted them to see that she valued their child.

When parents ask, 'Has he been good?', they are perhaps really asking, 'Do you like my child?' Jerome was pleased to see his teacher, but she made sure that she emphasised how relaxed and purposeful he was at home, what appropriate toys for his age he had, how she worried because he was always so beautifully turned out and his clothes might get spoiled for school.

By the end of the visit, the parents knew that the teacher sympathised with their work pattern and understood the need for a childminder, and that she obviously liked their son and was committed to working with him. They could trust her to be kind to him. She believed he was learning and she thought them caring parents who fed and clothed their child well and stimulated his development with toys. They invited her to visit again.

The partnership developed positively, through home visits. The teacher contacted the Ear, Nose and Throat specialist, who was very helpful in getting a different hearing aid with automatic volume control. Jerome began to wear it in school. Then the mother took a day off work to come to a coffee morning/talk that the teacher had asked the school's educational psychologist to give. She met other parents and enjoyed it, finding they had similar experiences and difficulties. At the next home visit, the teacher suggested to Jerome's mother that she might like to visit the classroom in action with one of the mothers she had particularly liked. In school the mother was struck by Jerome's speech when he was wearing his hearing aid. She watched the teacher working with the children, and took comfort that Jerome was showing off and in fact that her new friend's child was, too. All the adults laughed about it and the atmosphere was relaxed. Gradually the home visits became more focused on Jerome's learning, the curriculum, and care of the hearing aid. Ideas for follow-up activities at home were given. The parents told the teacher what they observed Jerome doing and the teacher shared what happened at school. The parents began to write in the home book. At six years, Jerome was beginning to read, talk and lip-read well and was a more relaxed child. He transferred to a partial hearing unit and a year later was integrated successfully into his local primary school, where his parents were able to give him the necessary support.

They trusted his teachers, respecting their knowledge, felt able to ask for help and information, felt included in his education, knew they were important, and that the professionals regarded them as good, loving parents.

The key factors in this successful parent/teacher partnership were that the teacher built up the parents' self-confidence and extended what the parents thought education was about, rather than displacing their view with something totally different. The teacher gathered resources and information through a multiprofessional approach, working with the health visitor, specialist doctor and educational psychologist. Not all professionals welcomed this contact (in this instance, the GP did not), but the teacher kept going until she found those who also valued a multi-professional approach. She put the parents in touch with other parents to form a self-help group, and used an away-from-school setting prior to encouraging the parents into school.

Where there is little or no contact between professional workers, parents can be left confused and let down.

Kaplan (1978) talks about the awakening of the unloved self in the parent in the case of a child with a disability. This may well also apply to the parents' relationship with a child at the toddler stage of temper tantrums. Parents need to feel supported, not undermined, by professionals.

JOHN

Two-year-old John's mother cared deeply about his healthy development. He attended a dentist as soon as his teeth came through. The dentist assured her that his thumb-sucking was not a problem. His mouth would need orthodontic treatment at 9 or 10 years anyway, and he was likely to grow out of it by five or six years. His mother relaxed.

When John started at a playgroup, staff discouraged him from sucking his thumb during story time. Mother began to worry again when John reported this. She did not like to mention it to the supervisor, who obviously knew more than she did (in her view). At six years of age, John was still sucking his thumb. At eight years of age, the dentist suggested a visit to the orthodontist in preparation for later treatment. She insisted that the thumb-sucking was no problem. The orthodontist greeted John with, 'And what do you do that you shouldn't do?', and was unpleasant to him about it, saying she would do nothing for him until he gave it up. John's mother ventured to say that she had thought treatment would not begin until he was 10 and that John now only sucked his thumb on going to sleep, or if distressed. The orthodontist gave a smile, but no information.

At the next visit to the dentist, the mother reported this back. The dentist closed professional ranks with the orthodontist, and said, 'Well, he's nearly stopped now, hasn't he?' John's mother felt confused about the conflicting professional views displayed in educational and medical contexts. She worried that as a parent she had failed to do right by John, but felt frustrated and angry because she had tried her best.

CATHY

Four-year-old Cathy's family was visited by a number of professional workers. The whole family was visited by a social worker and the health visitor called very regularly. The nursery teacher visited Cathy and her mother once each term as part of the school's home visiting policy.

The teacher and probation officer arranged for 14-year-old Paul to come in to school and work with his niece, Cathy. This bought out skills he could not use elsewhere – gentleness, patience, and so on. Officially, he was mending electrical equipment, which meant that he could hold his head high among his peers. The teacher, social worker and health visitor worked together on financial benefits, nutrition, and stimulating Cathy and her younger sister Sharon. Obviously areas of confidentiality had to be respected, but within that proper constraint the professional workers found that they could ask each other for cooperation and support because of the 'willingness of spirit' and basic trust that had developed between them.

Working as a team

When partnerships are strong, the different roles of practitioners complement each other.

Figure 9.4: A parent greets their child, who is playing in the sand outside.

Conclusion

This chapter has explored significant people in a child's life – some in the family, some outside it, some chosen by the child, some not. The ways that adults and children relate to each other are important, and both family and those in contact with the family are critical in the child's development. The more that professional workers in statutory and voluntary agencies concerned with the child's family/carers work together, the better for the child. Meeting a variety of other children is also important, so that the child develops the ability to form relationships, which may be deep or of the kind necessary simply to cope with everyday living together.

10 Diversity and inclusion

Introduction

This chapter is about the empowerment of individuals and groups, so that whether or not children and adults are in a minority situation, they have access to full lives. For early childhood practitioners this means helping children to have fulfilling lives, both in their home life and beyond. This means confronting discrimination and oppression of all kinds. One of the problems educators have always encountered is how to work with children respectfully and value them as unique individuals within a whole group. Even within the family, this can be difficult. A 'one-size-fits-all' approach does not work. Children are not all the same.

Policy-makers and educational theorists have, over the years, identified particular groups of children whose needs have been significantly ignored. As long ago as the 1960s, studies such as Douglas's (1964) alerted practitioners to the fact that working-class children were not being successful in the education system. This led to attempts to remedy the situation through compensatory education focusing on cognition. Three useful features emerged from the compensatory movement. Programmes with lasting impact were found:

1. to work in partnership with parents and the rest of the family;
2. to be geared to individuals within the group;
3. to be structured in a planned, well-thought-through and consistent way.

Because the whole family was involved, account was taken of what the child came to school able to do. The child's background and home experiences were valued. Observing the child and using what the child was naturally doing were also valued. Examples of this approach can be seen in Constance Kamii's work in the Ypsilanti Early Education Programme in the USA, the Halsey Studies on Educational Priority in the UK, together with the Leverhulme/Gulbenkian Froebel Nursery Research Project directed by Chris Athey at the Froebel Institute, London, 1972–77.

All children need individual and sensitive treatment, whether they are with childminders, or in group settings.

Guiding principles for early childhood practice

At an Organisation Mondiale pour l'Education Prescolaire (OMEP) conference in London (which took place in 1983), Yvonne Conolly spoke on the subject of the multi-cultural classroom in the early years of education. She set out important guiding principles embracing diversity and inclusion, which are adapted in this chapter.

Early childhood settings and the individual needs of children and their families

* Children need a sense of belonging and inclusion.
* Promoting a child's sense of well-being and self-worth is essential.
* There is a need to avoid stereotyping.
* Everyone needs to inspect their own values, assumptions and actions in the way they respect other people.
* There is a need to overcome the natural stranger-fear of people through positive strategies.

Inclusion does not leave people out, inclusion stresses a sense of belonging

Jim was able to use British Sign Language and oral language. He was profoundly deaf. He had attended mainstream schools and was at university, but he had always belonged to groups of deaf people at which he had learned to sign. He had friends who were deaf and friends who were not. His bilingualism helped him to develop close friendships with both groups. He said that with hearing people he often became very tired with the concentration and effort required to listen hard and to lip-read, especially in group conversations. He relaxed with deaf friends where he could sign. Interestingly, Jim's first remark when he met anyone at the summer school was, 'Are you deaf or hearing?' He was at ease with his deafness. He did not try to deny it. He did not want to. His only bitterness was that hearing people were so insensitive to the needs of the minority group to which he belonged. He felt a privileged member of his group, as he was bilingual. His parents had fought hard to help him succeed in spite of all the obstacles posed by insensitive and inflexible systems.

Inclusion: a sense of well-being and belonging

Everyone needs roots and to feel that they belong to a group. The inclusive approach can be seen in the need to value and encourage the child's home language where a different language is used from that used in the school. It is also present in the need to value dialects and accents that relate to class and regional differences. It is present in the need for children of minority ethnic groups to know about their own language, cultural roots and religious ideas, and for the educator to value these.

Floella Benjamin (1995: 121), writing about 'Coming to England' in her book, says, 'To feel you belong is a most important necessity in life.'

Three-year-old **PRATIMA** came to school with her grandmother, who spoke Punjabi. The teacher managed to greet her in Punjabi. Shortly after, Pratima became distressed and fearful. It was clearly something to do with her shoes and shoe bag. Grandmother could not speak English to explain to the teacher, and the teacher's grasp of Punjabi was too limited. Fortunately, the school was following an inclusive rather than assimilation approach, and Punjabi was sufficiently valued in the school for there to be a Punjabi-speaking member of staff. She was asked to help and the situation was instantly resolved. Pratima's tears vanished. The wrong shoe bag was on her peg; hers was found. Pratima's English was developing very well, but in a stress situation she could not use it and it would be inappropriate to expect her to do so. No one uses their latest piece of learning when under stress.

JAMES (two years old) was profoundly deaf; so were his parents. The family used British Sign Language at home and in their friendship circle. With his childminder, who was learning British Sign language, he was also encouraged to sign. She also used oral language and encouraged the use of a hearing aid. His home language was encouraged, but he was also learning about oral language so that he could become bilingual.

Like Pratima, James's home language was valued and encouraged while he was also introduced to English as a second language. It is important that the child's family feels included and belongs.

For individuals to be included communities must know about and understand individual and minority group needs.

HOLLY, aged four years, is growing up in a family with same-sex parents, Paula and Lucy. Her biological father, Matt, lives nearby and visits regularly. Holly attends the Reception class in a primary school. It is an annual tradition to make cards with the children to give to each mother on Mothering Sunday. At the weekly whole-staff meeting, discussion led to the conclusion that the tradition should continue, but that children who had lost their mother through death, who were in care with foster parents, or had same-sex parents should meet understanding and appropriate action taken to support their family context. Holly was encouraged to make a card for each of her two mothers.

Six-year-old **NAHUGO**'s mother takes her to school each day. She walks straight past the other mothers. This upsets William's mother, who feels her smile of greeting is rejected. A friend has recently returned from Japan and explains that in Japan people do not greet each other with a smile in the street. They ignore each other unless there is a verbal greeting. Next day, William's mother verbally greets Nahugo's mother. She looks a little taken aback, but immediately smiles and responds. Thereafter, the two mothers greet each other each day.

Families need to feel that they can trust those in whose charge they leave their children.

JUDITH was given pork at lunchtime in the early childhood setting. The practitioner who was her key worker intercepted, asked the dinner helper for an alternative meal without pork and quietly gave it to Judith. 'No one would have known', was the dinner helper's response. She did not worry that Judith's family practised Reformed Judaism, and that they trusted the staff to apply the dietary stipulations of the religion. On her course, working towards Level 3 qualifications, she became more informed and her practice developed.

Five-year-old **ANTHEA** attended a Church of England primary school. During assembly the head told the children about 'Doubting Thomas', who had the opportunity to believe in Jesus but did not take it. This placed Anthea in a dilemma. Her mother was agnostic; her father was an atheist. Both had had the opportunity to believe and had rejected it. What did this make her parents in the eyes of the school and church? Anthea dealt with the situation by keeping secret throughout her education the fact of her parents' rejection of Christianity as a means of retaining her self-worth at school. In fact, in many respects, she received a sounder spiritual and moral education from her parents than other children in the school. She experienced with her family a sense of awe and wonder about the universe (her father was a scientist). She learned about celebration at family gatherings when African music was played and danced to. She learned about 'worthship' in family gatherings, which involved discussion of matters of worth: starvation, poverty, peace, human rights and oppression.

This example demonstrates that organised religion, or belief in revelationary religions, is not the only means by which children are given a spiritual experience within a sound ethical and moral framework.

Six-year-old OVO's family were pantheists, believing in spirits in the trees and plants. He, of all the children in his class, was best able to understand the North American Indian tribes' relationship with their natural surroundings during the class project on this.

Five-year-old MARGARET was brought up as a Roman Catholic. She could understand that five-year-old Diana wore a Star of David just as she wore a crucifix.

Four-year-old SADIQ was taken to Westminster Abbey on a school outing. He thought the statues had no clothes on as they were carved in stone, and saw them as rude. His mother was fascinated by the outing and explained to the teacher, who was a Methodist, that in the Muslim mosque there are no statues.

All these children bring different experiences, although it is to be hoped that each will sense awe and wonder, and will celebrate and experience spirituality in some form.

Studying different cultures is a sophisticated, complex and multi–layered process. However, everyone eats, likes to present food attractively, uses crockery and equivalent tools to eat with, and sits in a variety of ways. Everyone sleeps, on beds, in hammocks, bunks, and so on. Everyone needs protection from heat or cold, resulting in a need for clothing, and everyone needs shelter. The different ways people tackle these aspects of life then become fascinating and important. They lead to respect for differences through geographical or regional variations, or for historic reasons, which help in understanding cherished traditions and rituals. They help children to see that diversity is rich, and to value the things that human beings have in common with each other.

Encouraging a sense of worth

Three-year-old NASREEN was from a Muslim family, but her father was an alcoholic and so her family was particularly disapproved of by the Muslim community. She had been brought to school as usual by her older sister. As the teacher greeted her on arrival, a neighbour brought his child in. He said something in Punjabi to Nasreen and mimed a drinking movement. As he turned to go she stuck out her tongue at his back and went to the practitioner and put her hand in hers. She knew the teacher valued her, and would not be judgemental towards her family.

The practitioner raised this at the staff meeting, and it was agreed the centre manager would discuss the incident with the neighbour, making it clear that this disrespectful behaviour was unacceptable in this community.

Self-worth, self-esteem and self-confidence are probably the most important aspects of human development. The way that people feel about themselves, their well-being, affects the way that they seem to others.

It is usually during middle childhood (8–12 years) that children become increasingly aware of their sexuality. This period is sometimes called pre-pubescence. Most children find their sexual feelings are towards those of the opposite sex, but a considerable minority, approximately one in ten, are attracted to the same sex. During the first seven years, children are establishing their gender and sex roles. In recent decades these have broadened in UK society as a whole. Half of trainee doctors are now women. Traditionally, men were doctors, especially surgeons. Fathers typically take an active part in childcare and household chores. Gender roles and sexuality are often confused. Because three-year-old Tom likes pink satin shorts and wears a ballet tutu with red tap-dancing shoes does not mean that he is going to be homosexual or a cross-dresser (sometimes called transvestite). It is important to be aware that being gay or lesbian is not the same as being a cross-dresser. It is easier for women to wear men's clothes than the reverse. The Turner art prize-winning potter in 2003, Grayson Perry, pioneered a trail for transvestites by wearing his party frock and wig, appearing as his alter ego, Claire, when receiving his prize at the award ceremony. 'Really I only want to thank one person, that's my wife Philipa, because she has been my best sponsor, editor, support and mainly my lover.' He was photographed at the ceremony with his wife and daughter, Flo.

One of the challenges of living in the UK today is when children bring their home prejudices into school. At home they may become inculcated with, for example, racist attitudes. Although very young children may not yet fully understand racist language they may hear at home, they might begin to use this in their school or early childhood setting. Value clashes in relation to disability, age, sexuality and race, for example, between home and school are challenging for practitioners to deal with. But these situations cannot be left with no discussion or actions taken (Lane, 2008). The vast majority of humanity does not wish to be racist, disablist, sexist, homophobic, ageist, and so on. Most of the time people act unwittingly, and when the situation is explained and pointed out, children and adults learn and change willingly. It is deeply disturbing for practitioners if they meet value clashes with parents in relation to diversity, inclusion and issues of equalities if those involved do not appear to be open to change. This is, however, not the norm. When or if this arises it is important to make sure that, within the setting or school, acceptable behaviour is insisted upon by the staff. Children learn different ways of interacting with people, and through reflection are open to change of values based within an ethical framework of respectful behaviour.

Four-year-old **KUANG**'s and six-year-old **MING**'s mother was British; their father was Chinese. Their parents helped them to understand Chinese culture through the furniture and decor in the home, the food they sometimes ate, the emphasis on stories and Chinese ideas about health, acupuncture, t'ai chi and herbal medicines. They also knew about the British cultural setting from their mother and from school. Kuang took pride in showing his friends how to write 'mountain' in Chinese. His parents helped him be proud of what he was: half Chinese and half British.

Avoiding stereotypes

Knowing who you are, and being at ease with yourself, is closely linked with self-worth. Part of being able to do this lies in the way children can put themselves into context. 'Who am I?' is an important question, which all people ask of themselves at some point in their life.

If children are labelled by others and stereotyped they are viewed narrowly by others, for example describing Peter as 'the blind boy', rather than someone who has as many qualities as any sighted child, or Ufoma as black or African, rather than a child who loves maths and hates gymnastics.

Helping children to identify themselves is probably the most constructive thing practitioners can do. It is important to avoid stereotyping people into an identity.

A teacher from Yorkshire attended a course in London. Everyone began to ask her about Yorkshire. 'Oh! You're from Yorkshire.' She began to feel that she was a foreigner. She felt her Yorkshire accent becoming stronger. She found herself wanting to read about the Industrial Revolution and the wool trade. She needed to assert her identity, but it was being chosen for her by others. She was swept along by the way that other people insisted on regarding her. She was being stereotyped as the delegate from Yorkshire.

It is important for individuals to assert their own identity so that stereotyping is avoided.

Later, at group time, she asked the children to look at the person next to them to see what colour his or her skin was. The children found a wide range. She stressed the commonalities and differences between them – all human, all with toes and skin, but with variations in the shapes of toes and colour of skin. She made it clear that she valued each child, and respected them all. She also made it clear that it was unacceptable that any member of the school community should not value or respect any other.

Mary's and Sadiq's mothers were both present at the song time. Both knew the teacher valued and respected their child, and themselves, and expected the same of them in the setting.

In a music corner, **BETTY** (four years) pretended to be the teacher. She held up a book to show the imaginary children in her class. Her friend, **JOANNA**, came and sat as a pupil on the floor in front of her. **JOHN** came and tried to join in, but Betty chased him away, refusing him admittance to the play. She seemed to allow only girls to join this play scenario. However, John returned, but sat at the edge by the entrance to the music corner. He stayed there and gradually moved forward bit by bit until finally he joined the play and was accepted into it by Betty. She had viewed his creeping towards the front with suspicion, but its slowness seemed to help her tolerate his gaining entry to the play.

Three-year-old **SADIQ** wanted to go in the home corner. The other children refused him entry. Three-year-old **MARY** said, 'we don't want Pakis'. The teacher heard, and confronted the situation directly. She told Mary that she thought her remark unkind, and that she did not want anyone in the class to be unkind. She asked Mary what a Paki was. Mary said, 'Black.' The teacher asked her if Sadiq was in fact black. She asked Mary what she was. Mary said, 'White.' She asked her if in fact she was white. She then told Sadiq to join the children in the house. They accepted him, and the teacher stayed and facilitated the play.

Overcoming stranger-fear with positive strategies

Mixing with a diverse range of people helps to break down stranger–fear, provided that positive strategies are developed that support the situation. Where children do not meet in a positive atmosphere, prejudice based on ignorance and stranger–fear persists, and can even be exacerbated. Attitudes to disability are changing as disabled people are more included than they were, although there is still much to do. Discriminatory behaviour based on ignorance and stranger–fear is not to be tolerated, even if it means unpleasantness in public (Siraj–Blatchford, 1994: 69; Lane, 2008).

Looking at our basic assumptions, attitudes, values and actions

Practitioners need to examine some of their basic assumptions about the way they introduce children to activities and tune in more sensitively to family styles of learning in order to help individual children in their learning. When children find familiar experiences and share these in conversations they have with the practitioner, relationships develop more easily and the learning is of a deeper quality.

It is important that the staff in early childhood settings meet and discuss issues of equality of opportunity, including ensuring the access of every child to become fully included the group. This will involve developing as a team a policy on diversity and inclusion for everyone to draw up together. It is also essential that every practitioner feels committed to this. Not only this, but a policy needs to be put into action and reviewed regularly to check that it is being implemented and to make changes as it is developed (Bruce, Meggitt and Grenier, 2010).

Attitudes that promote the guiding principles discussed in this chapter are of no consequence without action. Action requires commitment from people and appropriate resources. Practitioners need varying degrees of additional information, advice, support, special materials and amended environments if they are to work with principles of diversity and inclusion.

For example, the inclusion of a child with a visual impairment will mean extra specialist teaching support in the form of peripatetic advisers qualified in the education of visually handicapped children; additional technical equipment including Braillers; microcomputers with voice output; a special materials service of Braille books and tape-recorded materials; special lighting; and readiness on the part of the teacher to go for in-service training.

It is the practitioner's responsibility to press for the resources necessary to work inclusively with children so that rich learning environments are developed. It is important that support is given through relevant and effective training (through the Local Authority and SureStart Children's Centres). Parents need to be informed how to access information and advice and political channels (through their local elected representative).

Margaret Carr (1999) has developed 'Teaching Stories', which help the practitioner to evaluate what is offered to children. This makes a useful way of auditing for diversity and inclusion for childminders in home settings, or practitioners working in group settings. It is worded as if it is the child's voice, asking:

* Is this a fair place?
* Is this a safe place?
* Can I trust you?
* Do you know me?
* Do you help me fly?

These make a good starting point for reflecting on practice and thinking through action plans in relation to diversity and inclusion.

Conclusion

Ever since the education system was set up in the late 1870s in the UK, there have been debates about the extent to which education can change society, or whether it simply mirrors and reflects society. It seems that unless inequalities are acted upon at the macro level, fundamental change is unlikely, but there is much that can be achieved at a local level, too. The parts and the whole, the local and the society are interconnected and cannot function in isolation from each other. The key elements of diversity and inclusion principles are that communities of all kinds need to create systems that give equality of opportunity, respect and value to all who live within them. Attention must also be given to the various ways in which to empower children and adults as individuals, but also the groups who may be in a minority. This needs to be backed up with policies developed together as a team by those working with young children and their families, which are reviewed regularly.

* Children need a sense of belonging and to feel included, to choose their own identity and have a sense of self-worth.
* Everyone needs to inspect his or her own thinking and actions, and confront assumptions in moving towards diversity and inclusion.
* Fear of 'difference' impedes this process, and needs to be tackled directly.

Early childhood educators are in positions of power for breaking down narrow roles for children, or combating stereotyping of all kinds.

* All people have in common the fact that they are human beings.
* There is much diversity and many differences between people, but this is different from fragmentation of society or cultures.
* It is important to begin with what is common and ubiquitous to all people.
* Differences can be celebrated, respected and valued.

Everyone, child or adult, has in common the need:

* for a sense of belonging and inclusion;
* for a sense of well-being and self-worth;
* for a full life, not one that is narrowly stereotyped by others, with access denied or restricted;
* to overcome fear of people or situations that are different from what is familiar;
* to reflect on and look at the values, assumptions and attitudes that influence the way people act towards others.

Every early childhood setting needs a policy on which the whole team has worked and to which it is committed. This needs to be reviewed regularly to make sure it is actively carried out in practice.

Observation that informs assessment, planning and evaluation

Observation

Throughout, this book has given a central place to the importance of observation, using a variety of lenses through which to tune in to and understand the child's development and learning. This informs practitioners, working in close partnership with parents/carers, about planning next steps in learning that are appropriate for the child. It helps practitioners to plan effectively for the individual child, but in ways that ensure the child has a sense of belonging and feels included. The way that the child responds to what is offered helps practitioners to evaluate the appropriateness of what they have provided, which in turn leads to more planning in the light of this.

* **Assessment** monitors the way the child progresses in the setting, which may be home based with a childminder, or group-based. It is about tuning in to the child.
* **Evaluation** helps practitioners to interpret and analyse what they have offered and planned for individual children and groups.
* **Retro-forward planning** means we are always looking at what the child has been doing, is interested in, and has engaged with recently (retro) in order to inform ourselves about how to support and extend the learning and development appropriately (forward).
* **A record-keeping system shows the philosophy (the principles and values) of the setting in action**. If the record keeping does not reflect the principles the practitioners embrace, then there will be confused practice that constantly contradicts itself.

Figure 11.1: The boy with complex needs is with his key person during the group story time, so that he is included and able to participate, and so that the children in his group also enjoy the story.

The following principles of record keeping help practitioners to make effective links with the principles of the early childhood traditions outlined in this book. They also resonate with the core documents of the four UK countries.

Principles of record keeping that are in alignment with the traditional principles of early childhood practice (adapted from Bartholomew and Bruce, 1993)

The records need to:

1. keep faith with the bedrock principles of the early childhood traditions;
2. help partnership with parents/carers and be easy to share with them;
3. encourage children to reflect on their own learning;
4. be user-friendly, and make efficient, effective use of time and energy of staff, and easy to share with multi-agency colleagues and the child's future teachers;
5. use a variety of techniques for gathering observations, such as written observations, audio and visual tape recordings, DVD, photography, portfolios of children's learning;
6. link assessment of the child with evaluation of what the child is offered;
7. inform through sharing, planning and organisation, showing progress made and next steps;
8. link with current requirements of the day;
9. be flexible and grow formatively;
10. be capable of fine focus and able to yield specific information;
11. be easy to review and summarise;
12. show starting points as well as growth points.

In summary, records are about getting to know the child, and what the child is interested in and needs next. They show the philosophy and principles in action.

Evaluating the curriculum

Whereas assessment is about how the child makes progress, evaluation helps us to look at what we are offering a group of children or an individual child in the curriculum. This will involve practitioners looking at the experiences planned and the materials that they have used, and the way that staff and parents work with children, sometimes in groups and sometimes alone.

Some children find it easier to work in a small group, and on the floor, and free to move around. If sitting at a table is required, they begin to show challenging behaviour.

Figure 11.2: The children are playing with a truck. They are cooperating together. By observing one child, there will be plenty of information gathered about the way all the children participated.

Assessment and evaluation need to link together

Assessment (how the child is making progress) needs to be linked with evaluation (what the child is offered). When used together in a record-keeping system, the integration of assessment and evaluation by early childhood workers comes about through careful observation of children that informs the curriculum planning. Staff can begin to work out what they will next need to offer to children, either in a large group, a small group or individually.

Vicky Hutchin (2010: 43) suggests that there are three kinds of observation. Participant observations occur when the practitioner is involved in the play or the learning experience with the child. 'Catch as you can' observations arise when something significant is noted, but the practitioner was not directly involved with the child. Narrative observations are planned, and the child is observed across the day/week by all the staff, with the key person coordinating the observations gathered.

How to make a narrative observation

There are many different forms of observation, but narrative observation has been tried and tested across time since the 1930s when Susan Isaacs pioneered the method in her school, the Malting House. Her observations are written up in two seminal texts, *Intellectual Growth in Young Children* and *Social Development in Young Children*. The observations are as useful today as they were then. The difference lies in their interpretation. She analysed her raw data (her observations are through a Kleinian psycho-analytic framework. But any framework could be used. Narrative observations are typically analysed today through the official framework documents of the four UK countries. This gives practitioners and parents insights into the child's development and learning. It also deals with the accountability aspect in ways that do not cut across the philosophical base of the record keeping.

Narrative observation involves four steps.

1. The observer writes briefly about the context of the observation.
2. The observer writes down as exact a description as possible of what the child says/does. If other children are involved, the observer writes down enough description of the conversations and actions of the other children to give a clear picture of the target child.
3. The observation can then be analysed and interpreted.
4. The observation can be linked with the observations made by other people of this child. It can also be linked with official curriculum frameworks, research and theory.

This approach discourages value-laden judgements about families and children. It challenges the observer to reflect on cultural differences and to respect children and families, and to take inclusive action in relation to disability, special educational needs, and so on. The observer does not 'spoil' the data by analysing throughout. This is because the analysis comes at a later stage, after gathering on-the-spot description.

The description gives enough detail for the observer to be able to analyse this later, without making wild claims that are unsupported by the data. A particular focus can be given for the analysis, such as play, or communication, or relationships, or mathematics. When the analysis is linked to theory and research, it deepens and gives more illumination. It helps to understand and work with the child in ways that are right for the child.

Photographs and drawings are often included, and sometimes extracts of video.

Formative and summative methods of assessing a child's progress

It is simply not possible to measure most of a child's development or learning. We can only catch glimpses of a child's progress. Given this situation, it is damaging to a child's education if adults believe that it is only the learning thought to be measurable that is given any emphasis in the curriculum. It will bring about a narrowing of the curriculum where children are mainly taught to achieve on formal tests, rather than becoming educated in the real sense. This is sometimes referred to as the 'dumbing down' of the curriculum. It is the difference between helping children to jump through narrow academic hoops, with an emphasis on passive conformity, and expanding their horizons to provide a deep, rich and broad learning. The child will inevitably develop particular interests within this wider framework.

Formative assessment

Formative assessment methods emphasise the learning that children are involved in over time. The emphasis is on the everyday context in which learning takes place rather than test situations. Formative assessment is about the processes in a child's progress and the way children go through their learning experiences in the curriculum, gradually and over time.

Information is gathered continuously and regularly in natural, non-test situations; for example, collecting a child's paintings, photographing models, keeping examples of children's written efforts and notes about their dances or singing. The work on documentation in Reggio Emilia in northern Italy is explored by Edwards *et al.* (1998: 461–65) through guiding principles for practice, but only in the arts. The Learning Stories developed by Margaret Carr and Wendy Lee in New Zealand are also useful, and, in a different way to the Reggio approach, resonate with the early childhood traditions of narrative records built continuously to make a profile or portfolio, and developed in the nursery schools in the UK.

Narrative observation notes and photographs taken on the spot while a child is cooking, dancing, doing woodwork, using the climbing frame or hunting for ants in the garden are invaluable. These can be used to inform future planning. Vicky Hutchin (2010: 47) takes the view that 'Every observation is likely to have some implications for planning: first, with regard to the individual child and, secondly, for the staff and setting – perhaps changing a routine or introducing something new.' She suggests that, when thinking of the next steps for the child (the planning) it is important to consider what would help a child to extend their skills or understanding in relation to something they are observed to be engaged in. This might involve creating a learning opportunity, or resources. The way that practitioners participate with the child will be of fundamental importance too.

Thinking about how to support and extend the learning of one child might mean rearranging and adapting situations and materials, but Vicky Hutchin emphasises that this is likely to open up opportunities for learning for other children too.

Summative assessment

Summative assessment is about taking stock, pausing and bringing together everything known about the child's progress. Summative assessment can be staff and parents putting together key aspects of a child's progress, for example physically, mathematically, aesthetically or in terms of additional needs, diversity and inclusion or policy review. It is then necessary to decide next steps in what to offer and evaluate the impact of this on the curriculum.

Many schools and settings now have a 'special book' for each child, which shows both formative and summative assessment of the child through the child's learning journey. Significant markers in development and learning are entered, with photographs and examples of drawings, and so on, and annotations. These show the whole child (not simply literacy and number). Some examples will be gathered because it is realised they show particular aspects of the learning journey that have been spotted and deemed important to include for that reason. Some are there because parents have thought them significant. Some are chosen by the child. There should be contributions from key person, parent/carer and child. But there should not be clutter. Each entry should be there for a good reason, and the reason should be noted and dated.

Every few weeks (more often if the special book also serves as an individual development plan for a child with a special educational need or disability) a summative form will be filled in that brings together the overall progress made, identifies next steps and addresses any concerns.

Evaluation

Evaluation looks at what children are being offered and how this meets their needs, and it looks at what must be changed, adapted and developed. It involves a long-term plan and a medium-term plan, which are flexible, adaptable and constantly changing as observation of children informs the planning and daily plans emerge out of this.

Evaluation occurs regularly when staff reflect together on what children have been offered, and how effective the planning has been, based on evidence from observation informing assessment.

Using assessment, evaluation and planning in linked ways leads to practitioners becoming clear about their intentions and how they will act upon them, and to consider next steps in a child's learning. This means knowing about child development and the early childhood curriculum, and keeping up to date with recent research and thinking. In-service training is an essential aspect of this approach to evaluation and assessment.

Using both formative and summative methods of evaluation and assessment, education in early childhood supports the interactionist approach. Using one or the other does not, and has severe disadvantages. For example, one of the problems of the kind of summative methods involving formal testing is that what is measured quickly becomes what children ought to know. The problem of 'deriving an ought from an is' is called the Naturalistic Fallacy in philosophy. Assessment and evaluation are important to children and parents as well as staff. For example, at open evenings parents/carers often seize upon written work, drawings, paintings and models, or look for sum books. They want to see what their child has done and to compare this with what other children do. Parents enjoy 'performances' of music, drama and dance, because again there is a product to see, a tangible outcome. Outcomes such as these are often the only available means they have of putting their child's achievements, or their anxieties about their child's progress, into any kind of context. The anxieties parents experience about their child's progress cannot be stressed too strongly.

The advantage of using equally explicit formative as well as summative approaches is that parents and others, such as school governors, are included in the process of education, as well as the outcomes. They are helped to examine the education offered to the child beyond the superficial level, which tends to be entrenched in the education they themselves received. They can be supported in doing so by teachers who are confident and articulate, who constantly seek to improve the service, and are flexible in their thinking, which is based on sound conceptually based knowledge.

Parents can be helped to see a broad and more wide-ranging picture of the child develop over a period of time, based on the continual observations made, often by parents and staff, and on the plans formulated in the curriculum. Their involvement in this process working with the early childhood worker or teacher illuminates the process. Parents are then in a position to take pleasure in their child's strengths, and to tackle the weaker areas supported by the school or early childhood setting.

Seeing an individual 'interest book' develop as part of class work, or seeing different paintings displayed on the classroom wall and then made into another kind of interest book are examples of this way of working to make formative assessment more tangible and easier for parents to see in action. Parents are also able to see their child's progress in relation to other children in a more positive way than when suddenly plunged into an open evening, where the differences between their child's achievement and the achievements of others may be startling.

Records need to be kept of all aspects of the child's development. There are multi-professional implications in this. Health records are confidential, but of central importance for those professionals responsible for the child since the two aspects inevitably link.

Figure 11.3: The child is exploring tea leaves in the water with the practitioner. The child is taking up the initiative of the adult, but the adult is not taking over, as it is important that the practitioner is able to assess how the child is engaging in order to tune in to and support the learning.

Specialists of all kinds (medical, social workers, educational psychologists and educators) will need to share and build vital information together with the parent. Building records in a partnership can enable early diagnosis or monitoring of special needs, temporary or permanent, and indicate the level of support a child will need. This approach is particularly helpful in the field of health surveillance, and as a means of offering appropriate help in terms of preventive treatment, remediation or dealing with disability.

The teacher needs to observe and record how often he or she imposes control and discipline on the child, and to what extent children have self-discipline and can curb themselves. This is particularly important where a child has behavioural challenges. Recognising, appreciating and valuing children's efforts increases self-discipline, and noting progress fosters feelings of self-worth and well-being (Laevers, 1994).

Provided that good narrative observation techniques are in place and formative assessment is thorough, a child's needs can be met through using a wide range of materials. Drawing at a table might not appeal to a child, but drawing with a bucket of water and a large brush on the table outside might lead to very similar learning outcomes. The key is not to make the child come to the drawing table, but to take the drawing possibilities to the child, by building on what the children can do. Sharing such planning with parents makes them part of the team, with very positive results for the child's learning.

Narrative observation notes, photography, video tapes and collecting examples of models, painting, drawings and written work, help to capture the processes and outcomes of the development of symbolic behaviour.

It is as important to plot progress in dance choreography, musical composition and performance skill with a bat and ball as it is to see development in a child's written or number work.

Accurate assessment of children's development is possible only if work displayed on walls and in books is their own.

A parent at an open day said to **HARRY** (aged three years) 'What a lovely train. You clever boy to do that.' It was a template outline of a steam train that had prints from cotton reels on it. Harry said, 'I only did those' (meaning the cotton reel prints). The teacher had had the idea of making a train to fit a project on transport. She cut out the template and required Harry to print on it. She called this 'personalising' it.

All that this illustrates is that Harry can follow a simple instruction – and print on an outline – which is a very low-level achievement unworthy of the label 'creative' (Bruce, 2011a). Adult-dominated displays, although attractive, reveal a very low level of achievement that seriously underestimates what children can do.

In contrast, displays of work initiated and carried through by children, given adult support, demonstrate what children can do. The children's work can be beautifully mounted by adults and, where appropriate, explanatory notes about the contents or processes of the work can be given (since the result may not be obvious, for example a blob of paint on a page is representing a ball bouncing).

This method shows the adult's role as supporting and extending what the child can do (Vygotsky's zone of potential development), then sharing this through the classroom display, which illuminates the child's work but does not take it over.

Adults who help children to extend what they can do by themselves are more useful to children long term than adults who help them to perform through giving them easy props to lean upon in the short term. Deep down, children know the difference, and their self-esteem is enhanced if they feel real ownership of their achievements. The reward is knowing 'this is me being able to do this'.

Planning

Instead of making 'plans', which tend to be set in concrete, and are not changed in the light of children's responses (or, as is often the case, lack of response and engagement in relation to the plan), there has been a determination to engage in 'planning'. Planning implies a process, which is ever-changing, and that is exactly how things should be. This is sometimes called flexible, responsive or retroplanning. It means that the staff will map out ideas that, based on observation of children, seem to both respond to the child's interests and at the same time to what they need. The two need to be integrated. If children are not interested in what they are offered, they will not engage and learn. It is therefore effective practice to prioritise engaging children in what interests them. They are much more likely to be willing to struggle to learn something they find difficult if this is the case.

There are several things that need to happen, both at the same time, in synchrony, when planning the curriculum.

1. Analyse the observations of children across the week, and establish what is significant about their interests and needs.
2. Look at the official framework documents in use, and see what is in there that in any way links with point 1.
   a. Use large general points as the long-term planning. This might be an emphasis on personal, social and emotional development in the autumn when many children are new to the setting. This will not need to be changed very much, because it is more general than specific.
   a. Use more specific points as the short-/medium-term planning. Many settings now find they do not need both short- and medium-term planning. This is because they make good use of their observations. The child's interests and needs can then become the short-term plan, and can be incorporated into the medium-term planning.

In this way the observations become intertwined with the planning, both medium and long term. Getting the two together is the key to good planning.

One way of doing this is through PLODs (Possible Lines of Direction). These were developed in the 1990s by the author with Lynne Bartholomew, June Byne and the staff of Redford House at the Froebel Institute (now part of Roehampton University), and later taken up by the staff at Pen Green. They are now widely used.

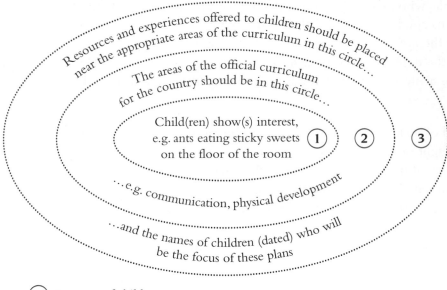

Resources and experiences offered to children should be placed near the appropriate areas of the curriculum in this circle...

The areas of the official curriculum for the country should be in this circle...

Child(ren) show(s) interest, e.g. ants eating sticky sweets on the floor of the room ① ② ③

...e.g. communication, physical development

...and the names of children (dated) who will be the focus of these plans

① Interests of children
② Areas of developing learning
③ Resources, experiences to be offered with particular children in mind

Figure 11.4: Planning for children's development and learning.

There should be planning for children, so that they develop and learn in ways that are right for them, at the right time for them. It should also ensure that children learn what they need to know, and are equipped with useful strategies for future learning, and dispositions that cultivate this. Planning should help children to find out about and deepen their possibilities to learn more about what interests them, what they need to know in order to function in the world, and what society thinks they ought to know as part of their cultural lives.

Summary

The lenses through which we observe children build on our understanding, so that we can help them to develop and learn as the unique individuals they are. We can help them to deepen their interests in worthwhile ways, and give them what they need.

The better our observations, the more they inform us and enable us to assess the child's development and learning so that we can identify and plan next steps. Observation also helps us to monitor and evaluate what we offer children in the learning environment indoors and outdoors.

The record-keeping systems we devise should be in alignment and resonate with the bedrock principles supporting quality early childhood practice.

12 The way forward

Ten principles of early childhood practice

1. The best way to prepare children for their adult life is to give them what they need as children.
2. Children are whole people who have feelings, ideas, a sense of embodied self and relationships with others, and who need to be physically, mentally, morally and spiritually healthy.
3. Areas of learning involving the humanities, arts and sciences cannot be separated; young children learn in an integrated way and not in neat, tidy compartments.
4. Children learn best when they are given appropriate responsibility, allowed to experiment, make errors, decisions and choices, and are respected as autonomous learners.
5. Self-discipline is emphasised as the only kind of discipline worth having. Reward systems are very short term and do not work in the long term in developing the moral and spiritual aspects of living. Children need their efforts to be valued and appreciated.
6. There are times when children are especially able to learn particular things.
7. What children can do (rather than what they cannot do) is the starting point for a child's learning.
8. Diverse kinds of symbolic behaviour develop and emerge when learning environments conducive to this are created at home, in early childhood settings indoors and outdoors.
9. Relationships with other people (both adults and children) are of central importance in a child's life, influencing emotional and social well-being.
10. Quality education is about three things: the child, the context in which learning takes place, and the knowledge and understanding that the child develops and learns.

(Bruce, 1987, adapted 2011)

The aim of this book has not been to prescribe how adults should work with young children. Rather it has been to provide a framework within which to work with some confidence that the approach will be consistent, balanced, and based on established theory and recent research. Detailed methods of work must depend on the individual practitioners and the teams in which they work, the way these are led and, most importantly, on the child in the family and the socio-cultural setting, and legal requirements.

From these principles, and taking account of prevailing practice as well as policy pressures (see the Introduction), the following action points are proposed.

* Adults need sensitively to tune in to, listen to and observe children. This requires better understanding of child development and of the different areas of learning. Graduate-trained early childhood teachers make an important contribution. Where they are found, the quality is deepest in early childhood settings.
* While emphasising the importance of being child-centred, there is a need to become more family/carer-centred.
* There is a need for better and more multi-professional exchanges, dialogues and integrated working between health visitors, speech and language therapists, teachers, family workers, and so on.
* It is essential to have a better conceptual articulation of what quality early childhood practice is, with appropriate assessment and evaluation, which does not cut across its valuable traditions. This requires highly educated, trained, qualified and mature practitioners.

The past leads to the future through the present. Heraclitis said (Collinson, 1987):

You can put your hand in the river once.

You cannot put your hand in the same river twice.

Bibliography and references

Abbott, L. and **Moylett, H.** 1997: *Working with Under Threes: Responding to Children's Needs.* Buckingham/Philadelphia: Open University Press.

Abbott, L. and **Arnold, C.** 2009: Schema and Emotion. London: Sage.

Abbott, L., Ackers, J., Barron, I., **Johnson, M., Holmes, R., Langston, A., Powell, S., Bradbury, C., Gooch, K.** and **David, T.** 2002: *Birth to Three Matters - A Framework to Support Children in their Earliest Years.* DfES, available from http://www.dfes.gov.uk

Arnold, C. 2010: *SCHEMAS and Emotion.* London: Sage.

Athey, C. 1990: *Extending Thought in Young Children: A Parent-Teacher Partnership.* London: Paul Chapman.

Baker, C. 2000: *A Parents' and Teachers' Guide to Bilingualism.* 2nd edn. Clevedon/Boston/Toronto/Sydney: Multilingual Matters Ltd (http://www.multilingual-matters.com).

Barnes, P. (ed.) 1995: *Personal, Social and Emotional Development of Children.* Oxford: Open University, Blackwell.

Bartholomew, L. and **Bruce, T.** 1993: *Getting to Know You: A Guide to Record Keeping in Early Childhood Education and Care.* London: Hodder Arnold.

Benjamin, F. 1995: *Coming to England.* Harmondsworth: Puffin Books, Penguin Group.

Bennett, J. 2004: 'Curriculum Issues in National Policy Making'. Paris: Organisation for Economic Cooperation and Development/Malta: European Early Childhood Education Research Association.

Blakemore, S.J. 2000: 'Early Years Learning. Report no. 140 (June)'. London: Parliamentary Office of Science and Technology (POST).

Bower, T.G.R. 1974: *Development in Infancy.* San Francisco: Freeman.

Bradburn, E. 1989: *Margaret McMillan: Portrait of a Pioneer.* London: Routledge.

Brennan, M. 1978: 'Talking Hands'. BBC's *Horizon.*

Brice Heath, S. 1983: *Ways with Words.* Cambridge: Cambridge University Press.

Bruce, T. 1976: 'A Comparative Study of the Montessori Method, and a Piaget Based Conceptualisation of the Pre-school Curriculum'. Unpublished MA dissertation, University of London.

Bruce, T. 1978: *Side by Side. Montessori and other educational principles.* Montessori Society AMI (UK) Third Annual Weekend Conference, February.

Bruce, T. 1984: 'A Froebelian Looks at Montessori's Work'. *Early Child Development and Care* 14, 151–173.

Bruce, T. 1987: *Early Childhood Education,* 1st edn. London: Hodder Arnold.

Bruce, T. 1991: *Time to Play in Early Childhood Education and Care.* London: Hodder Arnold.

Bruce, T., **Findlay, A., Read, J.** and **Scarborough, M.** 1995: *Recurring Themes in Education.* London: Paul Chapman.

Bruce, T. 1996: *Helping Young Children to Play.* London: Hodder Arnold.

Bruce, T. 1997a: 'Adults and Children Developing Playing Together'. *European Early Childhood Education Research Association Journal* 5, 89–99.

Bruce, T. 1997b: *Tuning into Children. A Child's World.* BBC/NCB.

Bruce, T. 2004: *Developing Learning in Early Childhood.* London: Paul Chapman Publishing Ltd/Sage.

Bruce, T. (Ed) 2010: *Early Childhood: A Student Guide.* 2nd edn. London: Sage.

Bruce, T. 2010 'Froebel Today', in L. Miller and L. Pound *Theories and Approaches to Learning in the Early Years,* London: Sage.

Bruce, T., **Meggitt, C.** and **Grenier, J.** 2010: *Child Care and Education.* 4th edn. London: Hodder Education.

Bruce, T. 2011a: *Cultivating Creativity: Babies, Toddlers and the Early Years.* 2nd edn. London: Hodder Education.

Bruce, T. 2011b: *Learning Through Play: Babies, Toddlers and the Foundation Years.* 2nd edn. London: Hodder Education.

Bruce, T. and Spratt, J. 2011: *Essentials of Literacy from 0–7: A Whole-Child Approach to Communication, Language and Literacy.* 2nd edn. London: Sage.

Bruner, J. 1960: *The Process of Education* (2nd edn, 1977). Cambridge MA: Harvard University Press.

Bruner, J. 1990: *Acts of Meaning.* Cambridge MA: Harvard University Press.

Bruner, J., Wood, D. and Ross, G. 1976: 'The role of tutoring in problem solving'. *Journal of Child Psychology and Psychiatry* 17, 89–100.

Bunting, J. (ed.) 2003a: 'She's Not in Real Life, You Know!' Learning Through Imaginative Play at Tachbrook Nursery School. Centre for Literacy in Primary Education (CLPE)/Tachbrook Nursery School, Westminster Local Authority.

Bunting. J. (ed.) 2003b: 'Can Write'. Centre for Literacy in Primary Education (CLPE)/Dorothy Gardner Centre, Westminster Local Authority.

Butler, D. 1980: *Babies Need Books.* London: Bodley Head.

Butler, D. 1987: *Cushla and Her Books: The Fascinating Story of the Role of Books in the Life of a Handicapped Child.* Harmondsworth: Penguin.

Carr, M. 1999: 'Being a learner: five dispositions for early childhood. Early Childhood Practice': *The Journal for Multi-Professional Partnerships* 1, 81–1000.

Carr, M. 2001: *Assessment in Early Childhood Settings: Learning Stories.* London: Paul Chapman.

Christie, J. (ed.) 1991: *Play and Early Literacy Development.* New York: State University of New York Press.

Chukovsky, K. 1963: *From Two to Five.* Berkeley CA: University of California Press.

Clay, M. 1975: *What Did I Write?* London: Heinemann.

Clay, M.M. 1992: *The Detection of Reading Difficulties.* Newcastle-Upon-Tyne: Heinemann.

Cockerill, H. 1997: Communication through play: non-directive communication therapy. Special Times. Cheyne Centre for Children with Cerebal Palsy, pp. 1–23.

Collinson, D. 1987: *Fifty Major Philosophers: A Reference Guide.* London and New York: Routledge.

Conolly, Y. 1983: 'Keynote Speech: A Multi-Cultural Approach in Early Education'. London: OMEP Conference.

Corsaro, W. 1979: 'We're Friends, Right?' Children's Use of Access Rituals in a Nursery School. *Language in Society* 8, 315–336.

Covey, S.R. 1989: *The Seven Habits of Highly Effective People.* London/Sidney/New York/Tokyo/Singapore/Toronto: Simon & Schuster.

Crown, R. 2004: 'Children and Pets: Child's Play'. *The Blue Cross* 135, winter, 16–17.

Dahlberg, G., Moss, P. and Pence, A. 1999: *Beyond Quality in Early Childhood Education and Care.* London: Falmer Press.

Damasio, A. 2004: *Looking for Spinoza.* London: Vintage/Random Press.

David, T. 1990: *Under Five – Under Educated?* Milton Keynes: Open University Press.

Davies, M. 2003: *Movement and Dance in Early Childhood* (2nd edn). London: Paul Chapman.

Dawkins, R. 1993: *The Extended Phenotype.* Oxford: Oxford University Press.

Dennett, D. 2003: *Freedom Evolves.* Harmondsworth: Penguin.

DfES 2004: *Early Support: Helping Every Child to Succeed (How to Use the Service Audit Tool)* (ref. no. ESPP34). London: DfES.

DfES/Primary Strategy KEEP 2005: *Key Elements of Effective Practice.* London: DfES.

Dombey, H. 1983: 'Learning the language of books'. In Meek, M. (ed.), Opening Moves. Bedford Way Papers no. 17, University of London Institute of Education.

Donaldson, M. 1978: *Children's Minds.* London: Fortuna/Collins.

Douglas, J. 1964: *The Home and the School.* London: MacGibbon & Kee.

Dowling, M. 2010: *Personal, Social and Emotional Development.* 3rd edn. London: Sage.

Drummond, M.J. 1993: *Assessing Children's Learning.* London: David Fulton.

Dunn, J. 1984: *Sisters and Brothers.* London: Collins/Fontana.

Dunn, J. 1988: *The Beginnings of Social Understanding.* Oxford: Blackwell.

Dunn, J. 1991: 'Young Children's Understanding of Other People: Evidence from Observations within the Family'. In Fye, K. and Moore, C. (eds), *Theories of Mind.* Hillsdale NJ: Lawrence Erlbaum.

Dunn, J. and **Plomin, R.** 1990: *Separate Lives: Why Siblings Are So Different*. New York: Basic Books.

Edgington, M. 2004: *The Foundation Stage Teacher in Action: Teaching 3, 4 and 5 Year Olds*. 2nd edn. London: Paul Chapman.

Edmund, F. 1979: *Rudolf Steiner Education. The Waldorf Schools*. London: Rudolf Steiner Press.

Edwards, C., **Gandini, L.** and **Forman, G.** (eds) 1998: *The Hundred Languages of Children: The Reggio Emilia Approach - Advanced Reflections* (2nd edition). Westport CT/London: Ablex.

Elfer, P., **Goldschmied, E.** and **Selleck, D.** 2003: *Key Persons in the Nursery: Building Relationships for Quality Provision*. London: David Fulton.

Elfer, P. and **Grenier, J.** 2010: *Personal, Social and Emotional Development in Early Childhood: A Guide for Students*, 2nd edn, London: Sage.

EPPE 2003: *The Effective Provision of Pre-School Education Project: Findings from the Pre-School Period*. DfES/IoE.

Erikson, E. 1963: *Childhood and Society*. London: Routledge & Kegan Paul.

Fabetti, R. 2005: 'Eyes and silences. Early Childhood Practice': *The Journal for Multi-Professional Partnerships* 7, 8–12.

Fawcett, M. 2008: 'The Role of the Mentor: 5x5x5=Creativity Early Childhood Practice': *The Journal for Multi-Professional Partnerships*, 10, 64–75.

Ferreiro, E. 1997: 'Reading, Writing and Thinking about the Writing System'. Conference Lectures on Literacy: from Research to Practice. Lecture at the Institute of Education, University of London, 13/3, 1997.

Ferreiro, E. and Teberosky, A. 1983: *Literacy Before Schooling* (translation Karen Goodman Castro). London: Heinemann.

Fisher, J. 1996: *Starting from the Child?* Buckingham/Philadelphia PA: Open University Press.

Forbes, R. 2004: *Beginning to Play*. Maidenhead: Open University Press.

Fox, C. 1983: 'Talking like a book'. In Meek, M. (ed.), *Opening Moves. Bedford Way Papers no. 17*, University of London Institute of Education.

Froebel, F. W. 1878: *Mother Play and Nursery Songs* (translation Fanny E. Dwight (songs) and Josephine Jarvis (prose)). Boston MA: Lee & Shepard.

Froebel, F. W. 1887: *The Education of Man*. New York: Appleton.

Gardner, D. 1969: *Susan Isaacs*. London: Methuen.

Garvey, C. 1977: Play. The Developing Child Series, Bruner, J., Cole, M. and Lloyd, B. (eds). London: Collins/Fontana-Open Books.

Geekie, P. and **Raban, B** (1993): *Learning to Read and Write through Classroom Talk*. (www.eric. ed.gov/ERICWebPortal/recordDetail?accno=ED365414).

Gerhardt, S. 2004: *Why Love Matters: How Affection Shapes a Baby's Brain*. London: Routledge.

Gesell, A. 1954: *The First Five Years of Life*. London: Methuen.

Gleick, J. 1988: *Chaos*. London/New York: Heinemann.

Gleick, J. and Photographs by **Porter, E.** 1990: *Nature's Chaos*. London: MacDonald & Co./ Sphere Books.

Goldschmied, E. and **Jackson, S.** 2004: *People Under Three*. 2nd edn. London: Routledge.

Goleman, D. 1996: *Emotional Intelligence: Why it Can Matter More Than IQ?* London: Bloomsbury.

Goodman, Y. 1984: 'The development of initial literacy'. In Smith, F., Goelman, H. and Oberg, A. (eds), *Awakening to Literacy*. London: Heinemann.

Goouch, K. and **Lambirth, A.** 2007, *Understanding Phonics and the Teaching of Reading: Critical Perspectives*, Maidenhead: McGraw Hill, Open University Press.

Gopnik, A., **Meltzoff, A.** and **Kuhl, P.** 1999: *How Babies Think*. London: Nicolson and Weidenfeld.

Goswami, U. 2007: *Cognitive Development: The Learning Brain*. London: Psychology Press.

Goswami, U. and **Bryant, P.** 1990: *Phonological Skills and Learning to Read*. Hove: Laurence Erlbaum Associates Ltd.

Graves, D. 1983: *Writing: Teachers and Children at Work*. London: Heinemann.

Greenfield, S. 2000: *Brain Story: Unlocking our Inner World of Emotions, Memories, Ideas and Desires*. London: BBC Worldwide.

Greenland, P. 2000: *Hopping Home Backwards: Body Intelligence and Movement Play*. Leeds: A Jabadao Publication.

Gura, P. (ed.) 1992: *Exploring Learning: Young Children and Blockplay*. London: Paul Chapman.

Gura, P. 1996: *Resources for Early Learning: Children, Adults and Stuff*. London: Hodder & Stoughton.

Gussin-Paley, V. 1981: *Wally's Stories*. Cambridge MA/London: Harvard University Press.

Gussin-Paley, V. 1986: *Mollie is Three*. Chicago IL/London: University of Chicago.

Gussin-Paley, V. 1990: *The Boy Who Would be a Helicopter*. Cambridge MA/London: Harvard University Press.

Hall, N. and **Martello, J.** (eds) 1996: *Listening to Children Think: Exploring Talk in the Early Years*. London: Hodder Arnold.

Hall, N. and **Robinson, A.** 2003: *Exploring Writing in the Early Years*. 2nd edn. London: David Fulton.

Halsey, A.H. 1972: *Education and Social Change*. UNESCO.

Harlen, W. 1982: 'Evaluation and assessment'. In Richards, C. (ed.), *New Directions in Primary Education*. London: Falmer Press.

Harrison, C. 1996: 'Family Literacy: Evaluation, Ownership and Ambiguity'. *RSA Journal* CXLIV, 25-28.

Hawkins, D. 'Remarks: Malaguzzi's Story, Other Stories', in Edwards, C., Gandini, L., Forman, G. (1998) *The Hundred Languages of Children*. 2nd edn. Westport, Connecticut, London: Ablex Publishing.

HMT 2003: *Every Child Matters*. London: DfES.

Holdaway, D. 1979: *The Foundations of Literacy*. Gosford, NSW: Ashton Scholastic.

Holland, P. 2003: *We Don't Play with Guns Here: War, Weapon and Superhero Play in the Early Years*. Maidenhead: Open University Press.

Hutchin, V. 2010: 'Meeting Individual Needs' in T. Bruce (ed) *Early Childhood: A Guide for Students*. 2nd edn. London: Sage.

Isaacs, S. 1968: *The Nursery Years*. London: Routledge & Kegan Paul.

Jaffka, F. 1999: *Work and Play in Early Childhood*. Sussex: Floris Books.

Jenkinson, S. 2002: *The Genius of Play: Celebrating the Spirit of Childhood*. Sussex: Hawthorn Press.

Kaplan, L. 1978: *Oneness and Separateness: From Infant to Individual*. New York: Simon & Schuster.

Katz, L.G. and **Chard, S.C.** 1993: *Engaging Children's Minds: A Project Approach*. Norwood NJ: Ablex Publishing Corporation.

Katz, L.G. 1993: *Dispositions: Definitions and Implications for Early Childhood Practices* (http://ceep.crc.uiuc.edu/eecearchive/books/disposit.html).

Kegl, J. 1997: 'Silent Children, New Language'. BBC Horizon, 3 April 1997.

Kellmer Pringle, M. 1974: *The Needs of Children* (2nd edn 1980). London: Hutchinson.

Kellmer Pringle, M. with Brimblecombe, F.S.W. et al. 1980: *A Fairer Future for Children: Towards Better Parental and Professional Care*. London: Macmillan.

Kenner, C. 2000: *Home Pages: Literacy Links for Bilingual Children*. Stoke-on Trent: Trentham Books.

Kilpatrick, W. 1915: *Montessori Examined*. London: Constable & Co.

Kitzinger, C. 1997: 'Born to be good? What motivates us to be good, bad or indifferent towards others?' *New Internationalist* April, 15–17.

Kohn, A. 1993: *Punished by Rewards: The Trouble with Gold Stars Incentive Plans, A's, Praise and Other Bribes*. Boston MA/New York: Houghton Mifflin.

Krashen, S. 1981: *First Language Acquisition and Second Language Learning*. London: Pergamon.

Krog, A. 2003: *A Change of Tongue*. South Africa: Random House.

Lane, H. 1977: *The Wild Boy of Aveyron*. London: Allen & Unwin.

Lane, J. 2008: *Young Children and Racial Justice: taking action for racial equality in the early years – understanding the past, thinking about the present, planning for the future*. London: National Children's Bureau.

Lane, J. 2009: 'Knowing what Racism is (and is not) – a Prerequisite for Putting Racial Equity into Practice in the Early Years', *Early Childhood Practice: The Journal for Multiprofessional Partnerships*, 10, No. 2:91–100.

Laevers, F. 1994: 'The Innovative Project: Experiential Education 1976–1995', Research Centre for Early Childhood and Primary Education: Katholieke Universiteit, Leuven, Belgium.

Learning and Teaching Scotland 2005: *Birth to Three: Supporting our Youngest Children.*

Liebschner, J. 1985: 'Children learning through each other'. *Early Childhood Development and Care* 21, 121–135.

Liebschner, J. 1991: *Foundations of Progressive Education: The History of the National Froebel Society.* Cambridge: Butterworth Press.

Liebschner, J. 1992: *A Child's World: Freedom and Guidance in Froebel's Theory and Practice.* Cambridge: Butterworth Press.

Louis, S. 2008: Again, Again!: Understanding Schemas in Young Children, Stella Louis, Clare Beswick, Sally Featherstone, London: Featherstone Press.

Lindon, J. 2003: *Child Protection.* 2nd edn. London: Hodder Arnold.

Malloch, S. and Trevarthen, C. 2009, *Communicative Musicality: Exploring the Basis of Human Companionship,* Oxford: Oxford University Press.

Manning-Morton, J. and **Thorp, M.** 2003: *Key Times for Play.* Maidenhead: Open University Press.

Maslow, A. 1962: *Towards a Psychology of Being.* Princeton NJ: Van Nostrand.

Matthews, J. 2003: *Drawing and Painting: Young Children and Visual Representation.* 2nd edn. London: Paul Chapman.

Matthews, J. 2011: *Starting from Scratch: The Origin and Development of Expression, Representation and Symbolism in Human and Non-Human Primates,* London and New York: Psychology Press.

Maynard, T. and **Thomas, N.** (eds) 2004: *An Introduction to Early Childhood Studies.* London/ Thousand Oaks/New Delhi: Sage.

McKeller, P. 1957: *Imagination and Thinking.* London: Cohen & West.

Meade, A. with **Cubey, P.** 1995: *Thinking Children.* New Zealand Council for Educational Research, PO Box 3237, Wellington, New Zealand. (British Distributor: Community Insight, Cheney Manor, Swindon.)

Meek, M. 1985: 'Play and Paradoxes. Some Considerations for Imagination and Language'. In G. Wells, and J. Nicholls, (eds), *Language and Learning: An Interactional Perspective.* London: Falmer Press.

Milchen, K. 2010: 'The Urban Forest School: Reconnecting with Nature through Froebelian Pedagogy, Early Childhood Practice': *The Journal for Multi-Professional Partnerships,* 11, Nos. 1 and 2:106–118.

Milchen, K. 2011: 'The Urban Forest School', In Knight, S. (ed.) 2011: *Forest Schools and Outdoor Learning in the Early Years,* London: Sage.

Miller, L. 1997: 'A Vision for the Early Years Curriculum in UK'. *The International Journal of Early Childhood Education*: OMEP 29, 34–42.

Miller, L. and **Pound, L.** 2010: *Theories and Approaches to Learning in the Early Years.* London: Sage.

Minns, H. 1990: *Read it to Me Now.* London: Virago Education with the University of London Institute of Education.

Montessori, M. 1912: *The Montessori Method.* London: Heinemann.

Montessori, M. 1948: *The Discovery of the Child.* Adyar/Madras: Kalakshetra.

Montessori, M. 1949: *The Absorbent Mind.* Adyar, Madras, India: Theosophical Publishing House.

Montessori, M. 1966: *The Secret of Childhood.* New York: Ballantine Press.

Montessori, M. 1975: *The Child in the Family* (translation Nancy Rockmore Cirillo). London: Pan.

Moyles, J. (ed.) 2005: *The Excellence of Play.* 2nd edn. Buckingham/Philadelphia PA: Open University Press.

Murray, L. and **Andrews, L.** 2000: *The Social Baby: Understanding Babies' Communication from Birth.* Richmond: The Children's Project.

Nash, J.N. 1997: Fertile minds. Time 3 February, 35–42. New Zealand Ministry of Education 1996: Te Whariki: Guidelines for Developmentally Appropriate Programmes in Early Childhood Services Wellington: Ministry of Education.

Nicholls, R. (ed.) 1986: 'Rumpus Schema Extra'. Cleveland Teachers, Nursery Nurses and Parents. Based on lectures by Chris Athey.

Nielsen, L. 1992: 'Space and Self: Active Learning by Means of the Little Room', Sikon (available from RNIB).

Nutbrown, C. (ed.) 1996: *Respectful Educators – Capable Learners. Children's Rights and Early Education*. London: Paul Chapman.

Nutbrown, C. 2006: *Threads of Learning: Young Children Learning and the Role of Early Education*. 3rd edn. London: Paul Chapman.

Ockelford, A. 1996: *All Join In: A Framework for Making Music with Children and Young People Who are Visually Impaired and have Learning Difficulties* Peterborough: RNIB.

Oldfield, L. 2003: *Free to Learn*. Sussex: Hawthorne Press.

Orr, R. 2003: *My Right to Play: A Child with Complex Needs*. Maidenhead: Open University Press.

Ouvry, M. 2004: *Sounds Like Playing*. London: Early Education.

Oxfordshire Creativity Project in partnership with 5x5x5=creativity and Early Education, (undated, circa 2009) Evaluation report, www.5x5x5creativity.org.uk

Papert, S. 1980: *Mind Storms: Children, Computers and Powerful Ideas*. Brighton: Harvester Press.

Pascal, C. and Bertram, T. (eds) 1997: *Effective Early Learning*. London: Hodder & Stoughton.

Piaget, J. 1962: *Play, Dreams and Imitation in Childhood*. London: Routledge & Kegan Paul.

Piaget, J. 1968: *Six Psychological Studies*. London: University of London Press.

Piaget, J. and Inhelder, B. 1969: *The Psychology of the Child*. London: Routledge & Kegan Paul.

Pollard, A. 1997: Reflective Teaching in the Primary School. 3rd edn. London: Cassell.

Pollard, A. with Filer, A. 1996: *The Social World of Children's Learning: Case Studies of Pupils from Four to Seven*. London: Cassell.

Pugh, G. 2004: The early years of learning. Early Childhood Practice: *The Journal for Multi-Professional Partnerships* 6, 7–18.

Pugh, G. and De'Ath, E. 1984: *The Needs of Parents*. London: Macmillan.

QCA/DfES 2000: Curriculum Guidance for the Foundation Stage. London: DfES.

Rice, S. 1996: 'An investigation of schemas as a way of supporting and extending young children's learning'. Unpublished M.Ed. Thesis, University of West England.

Riley, J. 1996: *The Teaching of Reading: The Development of Literacy in the Early Years of School*. London: Paul Chapman.

Riley, J. 2006: *Language and Literacy 3–7*. London: Paul Chapman.

RNIB 1995: *Play it My Way*. London: HMSO.

Roberts, R. 2002: *Self-esteem and Early Learning*. 2nd edn. London: Paul Chapman.

Rogoff, B., Mistry, J., Goncu, A. and Mosier, C. 1993: 'Guided participation in cultural activity by toddlers and care givers'. *Monographs of the Society for Research in Child Development* 58, serial no. 236.

Rogoff, B., Paradise, R. Arauz, R.M., Correa-Chavez, M. and Angelillo, C. 2003: 'Firsthand learning through intent participation'. *Annual Reviews of Psychology* 54, 175–203.

Rouse-Selleck, D. 1991: *Babies and Toddlers, Carers and Educators. Quality for the Under Threes*. London: National Children's Bureau.

Rousseau, J.J. 1762; 1963: Emile (translation Barbara Foxley). London: Dent.

Rubin, Z. 1983: 'The Skills of Friendship'. In M. Donaldson, R. Grieve and C. Pratt (eds), *Early Childhood Development and Education*. Oxford: Blackwell.

Ryan, J. & Paquette, D. 2010: Bronfenbrenner's Ecological Systems Theory (written for National-Louis University, available online).

Schaffer, H. 1996: *Social Development*. Oxford: Blackwell.

Sherbourne, V. 2001: *Developmental Movement for Children: Mainstream, Special Needs and Pre-school*. London: Worth Publishing Ltd.

Siraj-Blachford, I. 1994: *The Early Years: Laying the Foundations for Racial Equality*. Stoke on Trent: Trentham Books.

Smith, F. 1983: *Essays into Literacy*. London: Heinemann.

Standing, E.M. 1957: *Maria Montessori: Her Life and Work*. London: Plume Books.

Steiner, R. 1926: *The Essentials of Education*. London: Anthroposophical Publishing Co.

Steiner, R. 1965: *The Education of the Child*. London: Rudolf Steiner Press.

Stephen, C., Dunlop, A. and Trevarthen, C. 2003: Meeting the Needs of Children from Birth to Three: Research Evidence and Implications for Out-of-Home Provision Insight 6, Scottish Executive. Available from: http://www.scotland.gov.uk

Stern, D. 2002: *The First Relationship*. 2nd edn. Cambridge MA/London: Harvard University Press.

Strathern, P. 1996: *Kant 1724–1804 in 90 Minutes*. London: Constable.

Strathern, P. 1996: *Locke 1632-1704 in 90 Minutes*. London: Constable.

Sylva, K. 1994: 'The impact of early learning on children's later development'. Appendix C. In C. Ball (ed.), *Start Right*. London: Royal Society of Arts.

Tamburrini, J. 1982: 'New directions in nursery education'. In C. Richards (ed.), *New Directions in Primary Education*. London: Falmer Press.

Taylor, D. 1983: *Family Literacy*. London: Heinemann.

Tovey, H. 2007: *Playing Outdoors: Spaces and Places, Risk and Challenge*, Maidenhead: Open University Press.

Trevarthen, C. 1993a: 'Playing into reality: conversations with the infant communicator'. Winnicott Stories 7, 67–84.

Trevarthen, C. 1993b: 'The function of emotions on early infant communication and development'. In Nadel, J. and Camaioni, L. (eds), *New Perspectives in Early Communicative Development*. London: Routledge.

Trevarthen, C. 1998: 'The child's need to learn a culture'. In M. Woodhead, D. Faulkner and K. Littelton (eds), *Cultural Worlds of Early Childhood* London/New York: Routledge, in association with Open University Press.

Trevarthen, C. 2002: 'Origins of musical identity: evidence from infancy for musical social awareness'. In R. MacDonald, D.J. Hargreaves and D. Niell, (eds), *Musical Identities*. Oxford: Oxford University Press, pp. 21–38.

Trevarthen, C. 2003: 'Infancy, mind'. In: R. Gregory, (ed.), *Oxford Companion to the Mind*. Oxford: Oxford University Press.

Trevarthen, C. 2004: Foreword. In T. Bruce (ed.), *Developing Learning in Early Childhood*. London: Paul Chapman, pp. xi–xiv.

Tumin, S. 1994: 'Inspecting Prisons'. One of a series of lectures by distinguished speakers sponsored by the Sunday Times newspaper at the Royal Geographical Society, Kensington, London, July.

Turiel, E. and Weston, D. 1983: 'Act-rule relation: children's concepts of social rules'. In M. Donaldson, R. Grieve and C. Pratt (eds), *Early Childhood Development and Care*. Oxford: Blackwell.

Vygotsky, L. 1978: *Mind in Society*. Cambridge MA: Harvard University Press.

Weinberger, J. 1996: *Literacy Goes to School: The Parents' Role in Young Children's Literacy Learning*. London: Paul Chapman.

Wells, G. 1987: *The Meaning Makers*. London: Hodder & Stoughton.

Whalley, E. 1994: 'Patterns in play. The use of schemas theory by teachers and parents'. *Primary Life* 3, Autumn. Oxford: Published for the National Primary Centre by Blackwell.

Whalley, M. (ed.) 2001: *Involving Parents in their Children's Learning*. London: Paul Chapman.

Whitehead, M. 2004: *Language and Literacy in the Early Years 0–7* (3rd edn). London: Sage.

Whitehead, M. 2007: *Developing Language and Literacy with Young* Children (3rd edn). London: Paul Chapman.

Whitehead, M. 2009: *Supporting Language and Literacy Development in the Early Years* (2nd edn) Maidenhead: Open University.

Whitehead, M. 2010: *Language and Literacy in the Early Years 0–7* (4th edn). London/Thousand Oaks/New Delhi: Sage.

Whiting, B. and Edwards, C.P. 1992: *Children in Different Worlds: The Formation of Social Behaviour*. Cambridge MA: Harvard University Press.

Winnicott, D.W. 1974: *Playing and Reality*. Harmondsworth: Penguin.

Worthington, M. and Carruthers, E. 2003: *Children's Mathematics*. London: Paul Chapman.

Index